M000196365

Penguin Monarchs

THE HOUSES OF WESSEX AND DENMARK

Athelstan*	Tom Holland
Aethelred the Unready	Richard Abels
Cnut	Ryan Lavelle
Edward the Confessor	David Woodman

THE HOUSES OF NORMANDY, BLOIS AND ANJOU

William I*	Marc Morris
William II	John Gillingham
Henry I	Edmund King
Stephen	Carl Watkins
Henry II*	Richard Barber
Richard I	Thomas Asbridge
John	Nicholas Vincent

THE HOUSE OF PLANTAGENET

Henry III	Stephen Church
Edward I*	Andy King
Edward II	Christopher Given-Wilson
Edward III*	Jonathan Sumption
Richard II*	Laura Ashe

THE HOUSES OF LANCASTER AND YORK

Henry IV	Catherine Nall
Henry V*	Anne Curry
Henry VI	James Ross
Edward IV	A. J. Pollard
Edward V	Thomas Penn
Richard III	Rosemary Horrox

* Now in paperback

THE HOUSE OF TUDOR

Henry VII	Sean Cunningham
Henry VIII*	John Guy
Edward VI*	Stephen Alford
Mary I*	John Edwards
Elizabeth I	Helen Castor

THE HOUSE OF STUART

James I	Thomas Cogswell
Charles I*	Mark Kishlansky
[Cromwell*	David Horspool]
Charles II*	Clare Jackson
James II	David Womersley
William III & Mary II*	Jonathan Keates
Anne	Richard Hewlings

THE HOUSE OF HANOVER

George I	Tim Blanning
George II	Norman Davies
George III	Amanda Foreman
George IV	Stella Tillyard
William IV	Roger Knight
Victoria*	Jane Ridley

THE HOUSES OF SAXE-COBURG & GOTHA AND WINDSOR

Edward VII*	Richard Davenport-Hines
George V*	David Cannadine
Edward VIII*	Piers Brendon
George VI*	Philip Ziegler
Elizabeth II*	Douglas Hurd

* Now in paperback

RICHARD ABELS

Æthelred the Unready
Unready

The Failed King

ALLEN LANE
an imprint of
PENGUIN BOOKS

ALLEN LANE

UK | USA | Canada | Ireland | Australia
India | New Zealand | South Africa

Penguin Books is part of the Penguin Random House group of companies
whose addresses can be found at global.penguinrandomhouse.com

First published 2018
001

Copyright © Richard Abels, 2018

The moral right of the author has been asserted

Set in 9.5/13.5 pt Sabon LT Std
Typeset by Jouve (UK), Milton Keynes
Printed and bound in Great Britain by Clays Ltd, Elcograf S.p.A.

ISBN: 978-0-141-97949-6

www.greenpenguin.co.uk

Contents

To Ellen

Note on the Text

NAME FORMS AND SOURCES

One of the challenges for modern readers of the sources for and histories of Anglo-Saxon England is dealing with a plethora of similar-sounding unfamiliar names. How to spell these names is a choice that all authors dealing with this period must confront, as Old English contained letters that have since disappeared from the language. In this book, I have followed a naming convention generally employed in scholarly works which involves retaining the letter Æ, pronounced like the 'a' in 'cat', if it begins a name, but replacing other letters unique to Old English with their modern equivalents. Thus a name such as 'Ælfþryð' appears as 'Ælfthryth'. Modern spellings have been used for names that remain current, e.g. 'Alfred' rather than 'Ælfræd', and 'Edgar' rather than 'Eadgar', and for all identifiable place names. The reader might note that 'viking' is not capitalized. This is by intention. In the tenth and eleventh centuries, the word 'viking' was not used as a proper noun to denote a specific ethnic group. Rather, it referred to an activity, participation in an overseas raiding expedition, as I explain further in Chapter 3.

The primary sources for King Æthelred's reign also require some comment and explanation. The *Anglo-Saxon*

Chronicle, the major narrative source for political events during his reign (978–1016), is actually an umbrella term for five separate manuscripts in Old English and several others in Latin translation. The earliest of these manuscripts was copied in the late ninth century, the latest in the mid twelfth century. By scholarly convention, the vernacular manuscripts are identified by the monastery in which they were compiled or kept, and cited by the letters A to E. All of them share a common stock up to 891, when the lost archetype was probably composed at King Alfred's court and distributed to various monasteries. The texts remain substantially the same until the death of Alfred in 899, at which point they diverge, as chroniclers in the monasteries in which they were kept added notices of events of local interest. Three of the manuscripts, C, D and E, contain the same narrative, with minor variations, for the years 983 to 1022. The author of this self-contained chronicle, referred to here as the 'CDE version', has been identified as a London cleric, writing around 1023. I refer to him as 'the Chronicler' in this book. Manuscript A has only three entries for all of Æthelred's reign, the years 984, 993 (correctly 991) and 1001. They are important, none the less, because these annals are independent of and earlier than the Chronicler's accounts of the same events.

The narrative of the *Anglo-Saxon Chronicle* can be checked against another valuable written source: charters, documents that record grants of land and rights and privileges over land. Charters issued by kings are known as diplomas. By convention, Anglo-Saxon charters are cited by their 'Sawyer' or 'S' number, referring to the annotated list published by historian Peter Sawyer in 1968. Historians have long appreciated the value of charters for a wide range of topics, including royal administration, political ideology, legal practices, the Anglo-Saxon Church and even landscape history. Most Anglo-Saxon charters are straightforward records of transactions, written in a standardized format using formulas that help identify the monastic archive or royal agency that produced them. Some of Æthelred's charters, however, are atypical, in incorporating narratives explaining how the estates came into the king's hands. Because charters served as legal title to possessions, English monastic houses in the centuries following the Norman Conquest undertook to preserve them in cartularies, and it is only in copied form that the overwhelming majority of purported Anglo-Saxon charters survive. Unfortunately, the monastic compilers of cartularies, intent on defending the endowments and privileges of their houses, did not hesitate to concoct pious forgeries to replace lost charters. Even authentic charters were 'improved' during the process of copying to better support the houses' claims. Approximately seven dozen authentic charters have been identified for Æthelred's reign.

Law codes and legal tracts represent a third important written source. Æthelred was a prolific legislator. His law codes provide a window on to crime and punishment in Anglo-Saxon society in the early eleventh century, as well as the ideological claims of the crown. Æthelred's law codes are conventionally cited by Roman numerals 'I' to 'X' and referred to by the place that they were promulgated. 'II' is the Treaty of Andover and 'IX' and 'X' are fragments of either lost codes or, possibly, alternative versions of 'I' and 'V'. 'I' and 'III' refer to a meeting of the royal council at Bromdune at which a code now lost was issued.

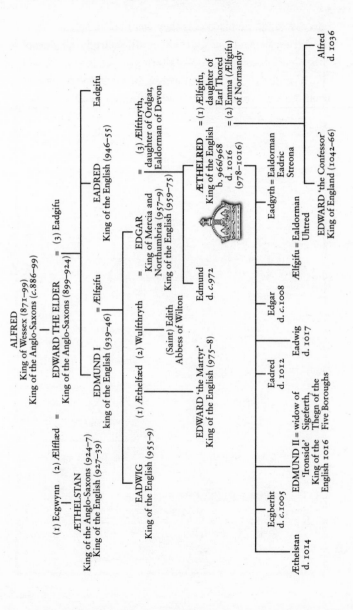

Aethelred's Kingdom

■ The Five Boroughs

0   100 miles
0   100 km

Bamburgh

N

Durham ●

Northumbria

North Sea

● York

R. Humber

● Gainsborough

Lincoln ■ *Lindsey*

● Chester

Nottingham ●
Derby ■ ■ *R. Trent*

Mercia ● Stamford

■   *East Anglia*
Leicester   Thorney ●

● Ramsey

Worcester ●   Northampton ●

● Olney-by-Deerhurst

Cirencester ● Eynsham ●
           ● Oxford   Maldon ●
        R. Thames ● Abingdon 'Assandun' ●

London ●

Rochester ● Sandwich ●

Watchet ●   *Wessex*   Canterbury ●
  ● Glastonbury   *Kent*
Gillingham ● ● Wilton ● Winchester

Shaftesbury
Cerne ●   Cosham ●
R. Frome   Southampton ●

Isle of Wight

English Channel

Æthelred the Unready

Introduction

Few English kings have had a worse popular reputation than Æthelred II (r. 978–1016), 'the Unready'. He is remembered, if at all, as the king who lost England to viking invaders. Until fairly recently, accounts of Æthelred's reign have focused on his unsuccessful attempts to counter increasingly devastating viking raids that culminated in two Danish conquests of England, the first by King Swein 'Forkbeard' in 1013 and the second by Swein's son Cnut the Great in the year following Æthelred's death. At least in popular memory, Æthelred 'the Unready' stands in opposition to his great-great-grandfather Alfred 'the Great', the latter as a symbol of English success and the former of failure.

Æthelred's byname, which has become so firmly attached to him that it appears even in works that reject its implications, is a misleading play on words that encapsulates the king's declining reputation. Like Alfred's designation as 'the Great', it was not a contemporary judgement. The soubriquet, a vernacular pun, is first alluded to in a work of the late twelfth century.[1] Names of the Anglo-Saxon elite were most often composed of two word-elements, which linked the child's name to those of his or her parents or a kindred group. *Æthelræd*, a name associated with the West Saxon royal dynasty, literally means 'noble counsel' in Old English. By the late twelfth century, and probably before, detractors were mocking Æthelred with a sarcastic vernacular pun on his singularly inappropriate name. Rather than *Æthelræd*, a prudent king who followed noble counsel, he was *Unræd*, a ruler whose policies were foolish or ill-conceived. The similarity between the Middle English noun *unræd*, poor advice, and the adjective *unrēdi*, ill-prepared, coupled with the characterization of Æthelred by medieval chroniclers as a slothful king, led to the gradual transformation of *Unræd* into 'the Unready'.[2]

The byname stuck because English historical writers of the nineteenth and early twentieth centuries found it an appropriate characterization. For them, Æthelred was the archetype of a passive, lazy ruler who preferred to purchase peace rather than fight for it.

Academic historians are by nature revisionists and it is perhaps unsurprising that the traditional view of Æthelred has been challenged. Recognizing that the main narrative source for Æthelred's reign preserved in the C, D and E manuscripts of the *Anglo-Saxon Chronicle* is a retrospective account written in the wake of the Danish conquest and tinged with the pessimism of hindsight, these scholars have highlighted the importance of balancing it with strictly contemporary historical evidence, such as royal charters, coins and law codes.[3] The result has been a much more nuanced understanding of Æthelred, one that provides perspective by balancing the narrative of military defeat with consideration of the positive developments that marked his long reign.

To view the England over which Æthelred ruled just through the lens of viking conquest is tantamount to historical tunnel vision. England was a wealthy country with a robust commercial and urban economy – which is what made it so attractive a target for vikings. It was also one of the most highly centralized states of the early Middle Ages, as evidenced by a monetary system so tightly controlled by the crown that coins were periodically withdrawn from circulation and reissued with new designs. England's shire and hundred courts and corpus of royal legislation, to which Æthelred contributed significantly, laid the foundations for English common law. The late tenth and early eleventh centuries were a period of ecclesiastical reform, and, associated with it, a golden age of Anglo-Saxon art and literary production. And contrary to his byname, Æthelred responded to the ever more dangerous waves of viking raiders and invaders with energy, innovation and flexibility, if not success.

No degree of apologetics, however, can alter the ultimate fact that Æthelred failed in the most basic duty of a medieval king, to defend his realm, although the blame for that failure was not his alone. Nor can it fully absolve him from the political violence and intrigue that plagued his court. Both were in large measure consequences of forces beyond his control: the fragile unity of the nascent English kingdom, the intense rivalries of the aristocratic families who filled the ranks of Æthelred's ealdormen and military commanders, and a hydra-headed enemy that grew ever more voracious. The challenges Æthelred faced in his nearly thirty-eight-year reign were serious, and, ultimately, he, his advisers and generals were unable to overcome them.

I
Martyrdom Most Foul

Æthelred II's reign begins with an unsolved murder mystery. On 18 March 978, the teenaged King Edward was killed while riding to visit his stepmother Queen Ælfthryth and her young son, the king's half-brother, Æthelred, at her estate in Corfe (Dorset). The murdered king's body was first buried without ceremony at Wareham; a year later the body was disinterred and brought to the royal nunnery of Shaftesbury, where it was reburied with appropriate honours. By the early 990s, reports had begun to circulate about miracles occurring at Edward's grave; shortly afterwards, an abbey dedicated to Edward 'the Martyr' was established at Cholsey (then in Berkshire, now in Oxfordshire) on a royal estate that had formerly belonged to the dowager queen Ælfthryth. In 1001, after viking raiding had become more intense, King Æthelred ordered that his brother's remains be moved to a more prominent location within Shaftesbury Abbey for reburial as a 'blessed martyr'.[1] Those who had martyred Edward, however, were never brought to justice.

The Anglo-Saxon clergy taught that lordship was the foundation of God's divine order, and that the highest species of earthly lordship was kingship. The murder of an anointed king was an affront to God and, in the years that

followed, the surly King Edward was popularly recon-
ceived as an innocent Christian martyr. The northern
version of the *Anglo-Saxon Chronicle* (preserved in manuscripts D and E) laments that 'no worse deed for the
English race was done than this was, since they first sought
out the land of Britain. Men murdered him but God exalted
him.'[2] Although contemporaries never directly blamed
Æthelred for the death of his brother, and the king was
among the chief sponsors of the cult honouring the martyred Edward, the murder cast a pall over his reign. In an
age in which divine explanations were sought for both
natural and man-made disasters, it is unsurprising that
some traced the tribulations wrought by the vikings to the
unpunished murder of an anointed king. Archbishop Wulfstan of York expressed this most eloquently in his 'Sermon
of the Wolf to the English' of 1014. The viking invasions
were God's just punishment upon the English people for
their multiple sins, the greatest of which were the betrayals
of two royal lords, King Edward to his death and King
Æthelred into exile.[3] For Archbishop Wulfstan the guilt
for King Edward's betrayal belonged to the entire English
nation. Post-Conquest Anglo-Norman ecclesiastical writers,
who similarly sought moral explanations for the conquests
of the English by the Danes and Normans, developed further Wulfstan's denunciation of the moral degeneracy of
the English nation. They, however, extended the blame to
the moral deficiencies of King Æthelred and, in the case of
Edward's murder, to the ruthless ambition of Æthelred's
mother, Queen Ælfthryth. The martyrdom became the
original sin of Æthelred's reign.

The historical context for the murder takes us back to the disputed royal election that had followed the death of King Edgar, Edward and Æthelred's father, in 975. Edgar's marital relations are murky and complicated.[4] Twelfth-century Anglo-Norman historians state that he was first married to a daughter of Ealdorman Ordmær named Æthel-flæd, whose nickname was either *candida* (white) or *enada* (duck). They thought her to be the mother of Edward.[5] The problem is that no contemporary source names either her or her father. Edgar's second wife, Wulfthryth, is better attested, because she, her daughter Edith and her cousin Abbess Wulfhild of Barking all became saints. Much of what we 'know' about her life, however, comes from late eleventh-century hagiographies. What we can say with some certainty is that Wulfthryth was a noblewoman, that she bore Edgar a daughter, Edith, in 963 or 964, and soon after became Abbess of Wilton.

Edgar's third wife, Æthelred's mother Ælfthryth, whom Edgar married in 964, is another matter entirely. She was the widow of Ealdorman Æthelwold of East Anglia, the son and successor of Æthelstan, nicknamed 'Half King' because of his extensive authority, and the daughter of a thegn (noble landowner) from the south-west named Ordgar, whom Edgar appointed Ealdorman of Devon soon after the marriage. Like Edgar's grandmother Queen Eadgifu, and unlike Edgar's first two consorts, Ælfthryth attested royal charters and played an active role in religious and political events as Edgar's queen, and even more so as queen mother during Æthelred's minority from 978 to 984. She is the first tenth-century English 'king's wife' to be styled queen (*regina*), a title which she seems to have enjoyed from the beginning of her marriage.[6] In 973 she was anointed and crowned alongside her husband at Bath. There may have been opposition to Ælfthryth's anointing from some members of the witan (literally, 'the wise men'), the king's great council of bishops, abbots, ealdormen (royal officials who would later be known as 'earls') and magnates. A preface attached to the rite used for the ceremony implies that Edgar ordered that she be consecrated alongside him. The author of the preface, however, made it clear that Ælfthryth was not being consecrated to mete out justice, as was her husband, but 'to the consortship of the royal bed with honour fitting to high royal status'.[7]

Whether others saw her only as 'consecrated to the consortship of the royal bed', Ælfthryth clearly interpreted her role as queen more broadly.[8] Unlike earlier royal consorts, she acted as an advocate in a number of lawsuits. That all of these disputes involved female landowners and most were resolved through the queen's mediation rather than by her advocacy in court suggests that she exercised power within the constraints of the accepted gender roles of the period.[9] Her most significant public and political actions were in support of the Benedictine Reform movement sponsored by her husband. She appears to have been particularly close to Bishop Æthelwold of Winchester, to whom she lent the services of one of her household officers to oversee the expulsion of the secular canons from the New Minster.[10] Edgar saw Ælfthryth as his female counterpart in reform. Just as he himself was to be the advocate of male monastic houses, she was to be the protector of nunneries. As reported in the preface to the *Regularis Concordia*, the Benedictine monastic customary approved by the Council of Winchester (*c.*973), Edgar 'wisely ordained that his wife Ælfthryth should be protectress and fearless guardian of the communities of nuns; so that he himself helping the men and his consort helping the women there should be no cause for any breath of scandal'.[11] The reformer bishops and abbots were fervent supporters of a strong theocratic monarchy and undoubtedly appreciated the value of having an anointed queen as protector of Benedictine nunneries.

Ælfthryth soon bore Edgar two sons, Edmund probably in 965 and Æthelred between 966 and 968, which immediately raised questions about succession. Edward, born to Edgar by his first union, was the eldest son, but some questioned whether he was the product of a legitimate marriage. That Ælfthryth, unlike Æthelflæd *candida*, was a consecrated queen argued in favour of the succession of her son. Ælfthryth's patronage of the Benedictine Reform movement and her role as legal advocate for all nunneries may thus be seen in the light of the queen's political manoeuvring on behalf of her son Edmund. Bishop Æthelwold became her strong ally.[12] Æthelwold's support can be seen in the characterizations of the queen and Edmund and Edward in the witness list to the refoundation charter for the New Minster, Winchester, issued in 966. This magnificent gold-leaf Latin charter is thought to have been drafted by Bishop Æthelwold himself. Edmund's attestation appears below Edgar's and Archbishop Dunstan's but above that of his older half-brother Edward. He is described as 'prince, lawful son of the aforesaid king', and Ælfthryth as 'the lawful wife of the aforesaid king'. Edward, who appears between them, is simply 'prince, born to the same king'.[13] (Æthelred either had not yet been born or was deemed too young to attest.) Bishop Æthelwold acknowledged Edward's status as an 'ætheling', a king's son, but clearly doubted that he was the product of a legitimate Christian marriage.

With Edmund's death in 971 or 972, Æthelred became his mother's candidate for the throne. Edward's claim to the throne was that he was Edgar's eldest son; Æthelred's, that he had the same father and that his mother was an anointed queen. Royal elections in the tenth century, however, had less to do with 'legitimacy' and principles of succession than with practical considerations, in particular the ability of the candidates to marshal support. The great men of the realm, lay and ecclesiastic, who constituted the late king's witan, chose the new king from among those deemed 'throne-worthy'. In eighth-century Wessex, this had meant any man who could claim descent from the sixth-century founder of the royal line, Cerdic. By the tenth century, the field had been narrowed to members of King Alfred's lineage. For the most part, consensus had not been difficult to achieve in the royal elections of the tenth century. This was not the case in 975, however, when Edgar suddenly died at the age of thirty-two, apparently without having named either of his two sons as heir apparent. The election divided the ecclesiastical and lay magnates. Despite Ælfthryth's support for monastic reform and her status as an anointed queen, the two archbishops, Dunstan of Canterbury and Oswald of York, favoured Edward's claim to the throne.[14] Bishop

Æthelwold, on the other hand, was in Æthelred's camp. Æthelred also had the support of the leading ealdorman in Edgar's court, Ælfhere.[15] Æthelwine, Ealdorman of East Anglia, and his brothers supported Edward, even though (or perhaps because) the queen had once been their sister-in-law. Through her patronage and legal advocacy, Ælfthryth had built up a clientele of influential abbesses and laywomen who also would have promoted Æthelred's candidacy.[16]

Ultimately, however, Edward was able to marshal more support than his half-brother. I suspect that the factors that proved decisive were Archbishop Dunstan's support and the relative ages of the princes. As Archbishop of Canterbury and Edgar's mentor, Dunstan's opinion carried great weight. Perhaps even more important was their ages. Although both æthelings were young, one was still a child. Edward was probably fourteen or fifteen years, about the same age as Edgar had been when he became king. He was a youth on the verge of manhood.[17] Æthelred, on the other hand, was at the most nine years old. To elect him was to opt for a regency in which the queen mother, Ælfthryth, would take a leading role. This may have swayed some of the clergy. One can well imagine Dunstan or Archbishop Oswald intoning the biblical lamentation: 'Woe to you, O land, whose king is a child.'[18]

Edward proved to be a weak and unlucky king in comparison to his father. The *Anglo-Saxon Chronicle* reports the appearance of a comet at harvest time soon after Edward's accession to the throne, which was deemed to have foreshadowed the outbreak of a great famine the following year.[19] The most dramatic event of Edward's brief reign was the so-called anti-monastic reaction, in which laymen attempted to recover family lands from the reform monasteries.[20] King Edgar had lent royal muscle to the Benedictine reformers' efforts to acquire landed endowments for their monasteries. The methods that Bishop Æthelwold of Winchester and others employed in this pious work were often heavy-handed. Even when the donation or sale was done freely, kinsmen of the donors might well have resented the loss of estates that they saw as family lands. As long as Edgar lived, disgruntled laymen had little hope of succeeding in a suit brought against a monastery, and even less of recovering the contested estates by force. Edgar's death unleashed the pent-up resentment, as the young new king lacked the stature necessary to maintain the peace. In the absence of royal authority, powerful ealdormen such as Æthelwine and Ælfhere protected the monasteries they favoured and allowed followers to despoil those favoured by their rivals.

So who killed Edward, and why? It is impossible to solve this 'cold case'. None of the versions of the *Chronicle* identifies the killers. Byrhtferth, a monk of Ramsey Abbey and one of the most prolific authors of the period, provides clues to their identities in his *Life of St Oswald* (*c*.1000) without actually naming anybody. According to Byrhtferth, King Edward was the victim of a 'wicked and treacherous' conspiracy concocted by 'zealous' thegns of his younger brother, and carried out by some of the great men of the realm. In Byrhtferth's narrative, King Edward, 'longing for the consolation of fraternal love', decided to visit his 'beloved' brother and stepmother at the unnamed royal estate where they dwelled. 'Fearing nothing and trusting in the Lord and the might of His power', the king took with him only a few of his household warriors. Upon arriving on the estate, Edward was greeted by the conspirators, described as 'magnates and leading men'. Byrhtferth explicitly tells his readers that Queen Ælfthryth and Æthelred were not present as they had remained behind. The unsuspecting king, still on horseback, was surrounded by mounted armed men, 'just as the Jews once surrounded our Lord'. While one of the killers, a royal butler, took the king by the right arm and made as if to give him a kiss of peace, another firmly grabbed his left arm and stabbed him. The king cried out and fell from his horse, dead. The conspirators allowed the corpse to be taken to a nearby house belonging to a poor man, 'where no Gregorian chant and no funeral lament was heard' and where the body was covered only by a cheap blanket. A year later, Ealdorman Ælfhere came to the makeshift grave accompanied by a large entourage. He ordered the king's body to be exhumed and moved for a more fitting interment. To the amazement of all, the body was miraculously found to be free of decay.[21]

There is no reason to doubt Byrhtferth's tale that Edward was ambushed by thegns of his brother on a visit to Queen Ælfthryth's estate at Corfe. Æthelred was king when Byrhtferth wrote the *Life of St Oswald* and it would not have been to his or his community's advantage even to suggest that the queen mother might have had a hand in Edward's death. 'Cui bono?' (Who benefits?) is a key forensic question asked by investigators of crimes. Those who stood the most to gain from King Edward's murder were Queen

Ælfthryth, her son Æthelred and their supporters, in particular Ealdorman Ælfhere. But the evidence against them is at best circumstantial. No contemporary source charges any of the three with the crime – even those written during Cnut's reign (1016–35), when it would have been safe to have levied that charge. One might argue that Æthelred's promotion of the cult of his martyred half-brother and Ealdorman Ælfhere's contribution in discovering and moving the murdered king's body are proof of their innocence. But they also could be seen as acts of penitential remorse. On the other hand, Æthelred's age alone – he was eleven at most when his brother was murdered – should excuse him as a suspect.

Byrhtferth's *Life of St Oswald* may not name the killers but it does suggest their motive. Byrhtferth's portrayal of Edward is inconsistent, to say the least. He is presented as both a Christian martyr and a brat. The account of the murder begins with a very unflattering portrait of the new king. Noting that Edward's election had been contested, Byrhtferth explains that many of the great men of the realm had preferred Æthelred as king because of Edward's irascible temperament, which 'struck not only fear but terror in everyone'. The king, Byrhtferth tells us, was particularly hard on members of his own household, whom he 'hounded not only with tongue-lashings, but even with beatings', which might explain the participation of a royal butler in the assassination.[22] Byrhtferth is often an unreliable narrator, yet I think that we ought to take seriously his characterization of the young king as an unstable teenager with an uncontrollably violent temper, not least because it clashes so sharply with his far more stylized narrative of the murder, which is clearly modelled on the biblical account of the betrayal of Christ. The magnates of the realm could not have been happy with the chaos of the 'anti-monastic reaction', even if they themselves were responsible for much of it. One can imagine that even those who had preferred Edward originally to his younger half-brother might have had buyer's remorse. The killers undoubtedly intended to place Æthelred on the throne, but they may have been motivated less by support for the child than by fear and dislike of the young king. After experiencing three years of Edward's outbursts of temper, many of the magnates may have preferred the 'more gentle' (and malleable) Æthelred on the throne. The murder was in essence a coup d'état.[23]

From the silence of the sources, it would appear that indeed no one was ever punished for the crime. This is remarkable on two counts. In Anglo-Saxon law, *hlafordswice*, betrayal of one's lord, was a 'bootless' crime, one that could not be compensated by the payment of a fine, and the killing of a king was the most shocking form that this crime could take.[24] Secondly, Edward's kinsmen did nothing to avenge his death. The ethos of reciprocity underlay morality and law. Even if Edward had not been a king, Æthelred, as his nearest kin, would still have been obliged to seek vengeance for his brother's murder. That he failed to use his power and authority as king to track down and punish the killers did not go unnoticed by contemporaries. The northern version of the *Anglo-Saxon Chronicle* pointedly states that King Edward's 'earthly

kinsmen did not wish to avenge him', but assures the reader
that his Heavenly Father revenged the slain youth by
forcing those who had killed him to venerate his bones as
a martyr.[25] Byrhtferth goes further. Comparing the murderers of Edward to the biblical Cain, which is as close as
Byrhtferth gets to assigning blame to Æthelred, he describes
how the killers 'flourished, passed out, got drunk, revelled,
because they were corrupt and disgusting to God'.[26] Like
Pharaoh, their foolish hearts were hardened by God so
that they would not do penance. God punished them in
this life as well. One of them, Byrhtferth relates, was struck
blind, a fitting penalty for one who would be deprived of
the sight of God in the next life. Byrhtferth assures his
readers that the others suffered similar tribulations as
divine punishment for their wicked deed. This was not
because the identities of the killers were unknown. King
Edward, as did all nobles, travelled with a retinue. They, at
the very least, must have known who had killed their royal
lord. That Æthelred as king never ordered his brother's
murderers to be apprehended and executed suggests again
the involvement of either Ælfthryth or Ealdorman Ælfhere, if not as conspirators at least as protectors of the
culprits.

Later medieval chroniclers had no doubt that Ælfthryth
was guilty. By the early twelfth century a tradition had
arisen that she not only planned the killing but executed
it.[27] The ordinarily reliable Henry of Huntingdon wrote in
his *Historia Anglorum* (History of the English, *c*.1140)
that he had heard tell that Ælfthryth personally stabbed

her stepson to death while offering him a cup of wine.[28] The late twelfth-century *Liber Eliensis* (Book of Ely) goes even further, turning the pious Ælfthryth into a harlot and a witch who murdered not only Edward but the first Abbot of Ely as well to prevent him from exposing her dark secrets.[29] This is the stuff of folktales. We cannot, however, dismiss the possibility that she was complicit in the murder of King Edward. Certainly, the killers must have had a powerful patron or patrons to evade punishment. For medieval authors who explained the disasters of Æthelred's reign as divine retribution on the English people for their immorality, it made sense to locate the original sin in Æthelred's accession to the throne through the murder of his brother.

On 4 May 979, at a large assembly held at the royal estate in Kingston-upon-Thames, Surrey, the two archbishops, Dunstan of Canterbury and Oswald of York, and ten diocesan bishops anointed Æthelred king, to the great rejoicing of the assembled magnates.[30] More than a year had elapsed since the murder of his half-brother, and three months since Ealdorman Ælfhere ordered Edward's corpse to be exhumed from its makeshift grave at Wareham and transferred to Shaftesbury Abbey for proper royal burial. Delays between the death of an Anglo-Saxon king and the consecration of his successor were not that unusual in earlier centuries when there were rival candidates for the throne, but an interregnum lasting a full year would have been unusual even then. It was especially striking in 978, in the months following Edward's death in March, when the only remaining ætheling was the child Æthelred. King Edward himself had tacitly acknowledged Æthelred's status as heir apparent by endowing him with the estates set aside for the upkeep of king's sons.[31]

The murder of King Edward, however, cast a pall over the succession, and the manner in which the killers disposed of the body exacerbated the situation. The sources agree that the killers mistreated Edward's corpse, although they differ on exactly what happened to the body. Byrhtferth says that the murderers allowed the corpse to be taken to the nearby house of a poor man where it lay covered with a blanket. The northern version of the *Anglo-Saxon Chronicle* states that Edward was buried at Wareham without royal honours. A late eleventh-century hagiographical work attributed to Goscelin of Canterbury, the *Passio et Miracula Sancti Eadwardi Regis et Martyris* (Passion and Miracles of Saint Edward, King and Martyr), meshed together the earlier accounts and embellished them with miraculous elements. According to the *Passio*, Queen Ælfthryth, who planned the murder, ordered that the corpse be hidden to prevent exposure of her guilt. Her servants dragged the body to a nearby hut, where it was covered with straw and then disposed of 'in hidden and marshy places'.[32] Nearly a year later, a pillar of fire was seen over the place where the body lay buried. Pious local men raised the body from its marshy grave and brought it to Wareham, where it was buried in the east end of the church. Hearing of the miraculous discovery, Ealdorman Ælfhere, to make amends for his role in Edward's murder, ordered the body to be transported from Wareham to

Shaftesbury Abbey and reburied with full royal honours. To the amazement of all, Edward's body was found to be completely incorrupt, a certain sign of his sanctity. This was the account that was probably promoted by the nuns of Shaftesbury. Archbishop Wulfstan, however, had heard a different story about the condition of the remains. In his 'Sermon of the Wolf', Wulfstan states as if it were common knowledge that Edward's body had been burnt.[33] It is difficult to reconcile these two early sources. All that can be said with confidence is that Ealdorman Ælfhere presided over the removal of a body from Wareham to Shaftesbury Abbey, where those remains were venerated as relics of a martyr. Whether that body was King Edward's is far from certain.

Miracle stories aside, it is unlikely that the whereabouts of Edward's corpse were unknown for almost a year. Certainly, the killers knew how they had disposed of the body, as did their patrons at court. It is more likely that Edward's body remained for a year in Wareham because there was no agreement among the magnates about what should be done with it. Those who had supported the assassination would have wished to delegitimize Edward and, despite his consecration, deny that he had ever been a true king. The dead king's supporters, on the other hand, would have insisted that he be buried with the honours due a king.[34] The latter camp claimed both archbishops. Dunstan, in particular, had been a key supporter of Edward's succession. He was undoubtedly horrified by the murder of an anointed king and the shameful treatment of the corpse. The prolonged interregnum may have been caused by the archbishop's refusal to consecrate a new king until the body of his predecessor had been interred with proper honours. If so, the reburial of Edward's body in Shaftesbury Abbey can be seen as a quid pro quo and a gesture of reconciliation, which might explain why Ælfthryth's ally Ealdorman Ælfhere played so prominent a role in the affair. The choice of Shaftesbury Abbey for the reburial may be significant.[35] Although it was close by, only about twenty miles or so from Wareham, the nunnery was not the obvious site for the burial of a king. Glastonbury or the Old Minster, Winchester, were more obvious places. One suspects that Queen Ælfthryth might have had something to do with choosing a nunnery under her supervision as Edward's final resting place. By transferring Edward's corpse to Shaftesbury, Ealdorman Ælfhere and Queen Ælfthryth acknowledged King Edward's legitimacy. They also appropriated his body.

But three more months after the burial of Edward would pass before Æthelred was crowned. The choice of Kingston-upon-Thames as the site for the coronation emphasized the legitimacy of the succession. Kingston, a royal manor in Surrey on the south bank of the River Thames about twenty miles upriver from London, had been favoured for royal coronations since Æthelstan had chosen it for his crowning in 925.[36] The sources do not describe Æthelred's coronation, but it probably followed the *ordo* devised by Archbishop Dunstan for his father's imperial coronation at Bath in 973.[37] That ceremony was replete with Christian liturgy and symbolism emphasizing the king's dual role as guardian of the Church and defender of his people: 'Saxons, Mercians and Northumbrians'. The three-fold royal oath that Æthel-red swore on holy relics embodied the clergy's view of Christian kingship. A king was to preserve the peace of the Church and of his realm; to forbid theft and 'all unrighteous things to all orders'; and to 'command justice and mercy in all judgements'.[38]

2

The Years of Youthful Ignorance

Æthelred was no older than twelve at the time of his coronation. Because of his youth, the new king probably had little say in matters of state. Rather, a de facto regency apparently headed by the queen mother and her two great allies, Ealdorman Ælfhere of Mercia and Bishop Æthelwold of Winchester, ruled in his name.[1] The return of Ælfthryth to political influence is signalled by the reappearance of her name in positions of honour in the witness lists of charters issued in her son's name. Unsurprisingly, Bishop Æthelwold and Ealdorman Ælfhere were among the first beneficiaries of the new king's favour.[2] What is perhaps most striking is how little the political establishment changed. With few exceptions, those who attested Æthelred's charters were the same bishops, ealdormen and even royal household men who had served his brother and father. The two archbishops who had supported Edward's claim to the throne, Dunstan of Canterbury and Oswald of York, remained important presences in the boy-king's court. Edward's murder had simply replaced one king with another.

The power of tenth-century English kings was limited not by political theory but by the necessity of ruling through and with the co-operation of lay and ecclesiastical elites. This would have been the case even if Æthelred had been of age and his succession had not been tainted by the murder of his brother. Royal governance centred on the person of the king. The power of a monarch was most directly felt in his physical presence, and one of the great advantages of itinerant king-ship was that it allowed local elites to see and interact with the king and his court in their own localities.[3] Royal itinerar-ies, however, were determined by the location of the king's estates and palaces, and those were concentrated in the south. Of the twenty-five meetings of the witan that can be identi-fied from the sources for King Æthelred's reign, only one was held north of Oxfordshire. In this Æthelred acted no differ-ently from either his predecessors or his successors, including the Danish kings Cnut, Harold I 'Harefoot' and Harthacnut, whom one might have expected to have held court at least occasionally in the 'Danelaw', the region formerly under Danish rule, comprising East Anglia, the east Midlands and northern England, that was distinguished by Scandinavian-influenced legal customs.[4] This made the loyalty of the ealdormen and bishops of Mercia, East Anglia and North-umbria all the more critical. Although kings appointed ealdormen, their choices, at least at the beginning of their reign, were largely limited to members of the great families. A true 'new man' was a rarity. 'Politics' took the form of competition among the great families for the power and wealth that came from royal patronage. A 'peacekeeping king' such as Edgar ruled in partnership with his ealdormen, bishops, abbots and leading thegns, exercising his power and authority effectively to support the Church, establish peace at home and maintain hegemony over the neighbouring British kingdoms.

In a sense, the child-king was a *rex pacificus* by proxy. The only major military action in the first years of Æthelred's reign was a ravaging expedition into Wales conducted by Ealdorman Ælfhere in alliance with one Welsh ruler against another.[5] The reappearance of small fleets of viking raiders coinciding with Æthelred's succession would look significant in retrospect but in the early 980s would have been seen merely as local disturbances of the peace. During the regency, the attacks on monastic property that had roiled the reign of Edward ceased. The trauma of the killing of a consecrated king may have played a role in the restoration of peace and order. From the near silence of the sources, England seems to have been well ruled during Æthelred's minority. The institutions of government that had developed during the reigns of Edmund, Eadred and especially Edgar functioned smoothly even with a child as king. The Church did particularly well, as the majority of grants made in Æthelred's name during the first few years of his reign were to monasteries.

The restoration of peace and the enrichment of the Church reflect not only the political influence of Bishop Æthelwold and archbishops Dunstan and Oswald, but that of Queen Ælfthryth as well. Edgar had rewarded his wife's support of monastic reform by making her the legal advocate for all the realm's nunneries, a role that she embraced. Belying the posthumous caricature of her as the wicked stepmother, Ælfthryth had consistently been one of the most ardent lay supporters of monastic reform. In this new political landscape, those who had taken advantage of King Edward's weakness to seize land from the monasteries now had to make their amends. Æthelwold's hagiographer Wulfstan the Cantor, writing in 996 or soon after, relates how the enemies of Bishop Æthelwold came to Winchester during the rededication of the Old Minster in 980 to make peace with the bishop by bowing their heads to him, echoing the ceremony by which a man commended himself to a lord – that is, became his retainer – kissing his right hand and asking for his blessing.[6] One suspects that this type of reconciliation was not uncommon in the first years of Æthelred's reign. In terms of the monastic reform movement, Æthelred's minority represented a return to the policies of his father.

This changed in 984. On the first of August that year, Bishop Æthelwold died. Ealdorman Ælfhere had passed away the previous year. The removal of these two strong influences freed Æthelred, now around sixteen years old, to announce his coming of age by taking personal control of the royal government. His declaration of independence apparently extended to his mother, as she disappears from the witness lists of charters between 985 and 993. Others fell from royal favour at this time. At a synodal council held at Cirencester early in 985, Ealdorman Ælfhere's brother-in-law and successor in Mercia, Ælfric *cild* (a term denoting that he was a youth of noble birth) was exiled 'by the unanimous legal counsel and most just judgement of the bishops, ealdormen and all the magnates of the kingdom'.[7] Although the ostensible reason for his exile was the 'many and unheard of crimes against God and my royal rule' that

he had committed, including the unjust seizure of heredi-
tary lands, Levi Roach, Æthelred's most recent biographer,
is probably right in suspecting that 'the ealdorman's fault
lay in opposing the king's new politics'.[8]

If some fell, others rose. Freed from the tutelage of his
mother, Ealdorman Ælfhere and Bishop Æthelwold, the
young king reshaped the court by using his royal prerog-
ative to endow loyal followers with lands and offices. The
charters Æthelred issued between 984 and 990 are anom-
alous in his reign as heavily favouring laymen. Æthelred
also reshaped the political landscape by strategic inaction.
The great ealdormanry of Mercia lay vacant between the
exile of Ælfric *cild* in 985 and the appointment of Leofwine
in 994, perhaps in response to concerns over the power
that Ælfhere had exercised. Æthelred broke with tradition
by *not* appointing the sons of ealdormen to their fathers'
offices. This has the marks of a deliberate policy aimed
at reducing the regional power of the great families and
asserting the king's control over the institutions of governance.[9] Æthelred seems to have been more comfortable
dealing with his reeves (lower-ranking royal officials), who
came from less powerful families. In 995 the Ealdorman of
Essex, Leofsige, brought charges against two royal reeves
for having allowed Christian burial for a man who had
died defending a thief. The ealdorman had the law on his
side, but the king found in favour of the reeves.[10]

Granting lands to favourites was not unique to Æthelred;
the ethos of reciprocity demanded that kings be generous
benefactors, and land was the most generous gift a king
could bestow. Some of the estates that Æthelred gave to his

followers, however, were taken from Benedictine houses in what amounted to a lesser and very localized second 'anti-monastic reaction'. As we shall see, a penitent Æthelred would look back upon these years as a time of youthful folly during which he had allowed unworthy, greedy advisers to take advantage of his inexperience to lead him astray. The death of Bishop Æthelwold deprived the monks of Abingdon Abbey and the Old Minster, Winchester, of their most important protector. Abingdon was rendered even more vulnerable by the death of its abbot, Osgar, a few months before Æthelwold's passing. Two new royal favourites, Ealdorman Ælfric of Hampshire and Bishop Wulfgar of Ramsbury, took advantage of the king's youth to exploit the situation. The bishop and ealdorman, in the words of the charter, persuaded the king to reduce into servitude the 'liberty' of Abingdon Abbey. What this entailed was an act of simony: Æthelred had accepted money from Ealdorman Ælfric to secure the abbacy for his brother Eadwine, in defiance of the privilege of free election granted to the abbey by King Eadred and confirmed by King Edgar. Abbot Eadwine and Ealdorman Ælfric used the abbey's lands to enrich their own followers. The king compounded this offence by taking estates belonging to Abingdon and the Old Minster, Winchester, and granting them by charter to favoured thegns. A notable beneficiary was Ealdorman Ælfric's son Ælfgar, who not only asked for and received church lands, but even gave land he had taken from Abingdon to his wife.[11]

King Æthelred's treatment of the church of Rochester was considerably harsher. The *Anglo-Saxon Chronicle* laconically reports that in 986 King Æthelred 'laid waste' (*fordyde*) the diocese of Rochester.[12] The *Chronicle* does not explain what Bishop Ælfstan had done to so anger the king. The Benedictine monk Sulcard of Westminster, writing circa 1080, attributes it to a property dispute.[13] According to Sulcard, King Æthelred had acceded to the request of one of his thegns, Æthelsige, for an estate that belonged to the Bishop of Rochester. The bishop, who had not been consulted, forcefully evicted the thegn. The king's response was to attack the city of Rochester and harry the lands belonging to the bishop, a response not dissimilar to that of his father to his disobedient subjects of Thanet in 969. The effects of the harrying of the diocese can be seen in the disruption of production of coins by Rochester's mint.[14] Archbishop Dunstan, according to Sulcard, reproved the king for having acted illegally in giving Rochester's lands to his thegn and in a high-handed manner in ravaging the diocese, but the king just grew angrier.[15] Bishop Ælfstan seems to have prudently withdrawn from the court, as he ceases to attest royal charters in 984 and does not reappear until 988.

But one should not see this period as a broad attack upon Benedictine monastic houses. The despoliation was localized. During these years, Æthelweard, Ealdorman of the 'Western Provinces', who was to gain fame for his Latin rendering of the *Anglo-Saxon Chronicle*, and his son Æthelmær the Stout promoted the Benedictine movement in the shires of Dorset, Somerset and Devon.[16] Ealdorman Byrhtnoth of Essex remained the protector of Ely Abbey in Cambridgeshire, while Ealdorman Æthelwine of East Anglia, son and successor of Æthelstan 'Half

King', continued his father's patronage of the monasteries of Glastonbury and Ramsey. It is probably not coincidental that two of the three religious houses targeted were associated with Bishop Æthelwold. As with the 'anti-monastic reaction' of Edward the Martyr's reign, the appropriation of church lands should probably be understood as rooted in opportunism.

Æthelred announced his entry into manhood by choosing a wife. It is not known exactly when Æthelred married, but it was probably around 984/5 and no later than 989, as four of the king's sons appear in the witness list of a charter issued in 993. Æthelred's first wife is not named in any contemporary sources. Unlike Queen Ælfthryth, she attests no charters. Anglo-Norman historians give her name as Ælfgifu and report that she was the daughter of 'Earl Thored', who was the Ealdorman of York in the 980s.[17] This is plausible if not certain. The match would have made political sense as a means of extending the king's influence over Northumbria, the most remote part of his realm. If 'Queen Ælfgifu' has left no political imprint of her own, she was successful in the activity most critical for a royal consort: bearing children. The union produced six sons – Æthelstan, Ecgbert, Edmund, Eadred, Eadwig, Edgar – and two daughters. With the exception of his second son, Æthelred named his sons after his predecessors on the throne in order of their succession, beginning with the then most prestigious ruler of his dynasty. When he married his second wife, the Norman princess Emma, in 1002, he continued the practice by naming the first of his two sons by her Edward. For the second he had to turn

back to Alfred. His daughters were named after his pater-
nal grandmother Ælfgifu and his half-sister Eadgyth, both
of whom were venerated as saints. These names emphasized dynastic continuity and Æthelred's royal lineage.

If the early years of Æthelred's personal rule differed
from the reign of his father in his treatment of monasteries,
they also differed in another respect. King Edgar's poetic
obituary in the DE version of the *Anglo-Saxon Chronicle*,
probably composed by Archbishop Wulfstan of York in the
second half of Æthelred's reign, remembered the king's rule
as a time when 'there was no fleet so proud, nor raiding-
army so strong, that fetched itself carrion among the
English race'.[18] Within a year of Æthelred's coronation, this
boast could no longer be made. In the autumn of 980, the
borough of Southampton was sacked by a viking fleet of
seven ships.[19] The C version of the *Chronicle* adds that
most of the townspeople were killed or taken prisoner. In
that same year, the Isle of Thanet and the northern coast of
Cheshire were also the targets of raids. This was the beginning of a series of sporadic coastal viking incursions in the
980s. The raiding intensified the following year, as vikings
attacked 'St. Petrock's holy place' (presumably Padstow on
the northern coast of Cornwall), and 'great harm was done
everywhere along the sea-coast, both in Devon and Cornwall'.[20] In 982 three viking ships ravaged Portland in
Dorset. The only battle that we hear of occurred in 988,
when a local militia apparently consisting of levies from
Somerset and Devon engaged a viking force that after pillaging five monasteries in southern Wales sacked Watchet
on the north coast of Somerset, an Alfredian fortified town

that had become the site of a mint by the late tenth century. The *Chronicle* reports that a Devonshire thegn named Goda was killed in the battle, and many fell with him, although it fails to say which side won the battle.[21] The engagement was of sufficient significance to draw the attention of Byrhtferth at Ramsey, who treated it as a hard-fought victory. Although the English lost many men, including 'a valiant soldier named Stremwold', Byrhtferth assured the reader that the Danes lost even more.[22]

Viking activity in Britain and France had all but ceased during the four decades preceding the sack of Southampton. That some viking raiding – or at least the threat of raids – continued during these decades, however, is evidenced by the considerable sum of £1,600 that Æthelred's uncle King Eadred had entrusted in his will (drawn up some time between 951 and 955) to his bishops to be used for relief of famine and 'to buy off a heathen raiding army, if the need arose'.[23] Both seem to have been real possibilities in the early 950s. More certainly, the Scandinavian chieftains of the Isle of Man, the Orkneys and the Hebrides, as well as adventurers from Ireland, continued the traditional viking way of life by ravaging coastal towns and monasteries in Ireland, Scotland and Wales in the second half of the tenth century.[24] The sporadic raiding along the southwestern coast of England in the 980s was probably simply an extension of the viking activity that had continued in the Irish Sea.

The attacks on Southampton and Thanet may have originated in Scandinavia. Certainly, the large fleet that descended upon England in 991 did. One can only speculate why viking raids from Norway and Denmark began again in the 980s. Undoubtedly, the promise of wealth was a major factor, as it had been a century earlier. England in the late tenth century was a prosperous country, as Scandinavians would have known from reports by merchants and travellers. Archbishop Wulfstan located the roots of the viking problem of his day in the openness and hospitality of King Edgar's court. He concluded an otherwise laudatory summary of Edgar's reign in the *Anglo-Saxon Chronicle* with some rueful criticism: 'One evil deed, however, he did too much, in that he loved bad, foreign habits, and brought heathen customs too firmly into this land *and attracted the foreigner here, and introduced a damaging people into this country.*'[25] A rich country ruled by a child-king was sufficient enticement to revive the viking spirit. Political developments within Scandinavia contributed as well, with a child-king playing a role there too. Denmark's first Christian king, Harald 'Bluetooth' (r. 958–87), had been preoccupied for most of his reign with state-building, imposing Danish hegemony over the coastal regions of southern Norway and Sweden, and defending his southern border from German invasion.[26] The German threat ended with the death of Emperor Otto II in 983 and the accession of his three-year-old son. Meanwhile, unstable political conditions in Norway and Sweden encouraged would-be kings and ambitious jarls (earls) to go a-viking in pursuit of wealth to fund political ambitions at home.

The small-scale raiding of the 980s was a matter of local concern. In 991 a viking fleet of an entirely different order of magnitude landed at Folkestone, Kent.[27] After sacking the coastal towns of Sandwich and Ipswich, the vikings turned towards Maldon in Essex. There they were met by local forces from Essex led by the venerable Ealdorman Byrhtnoth. The battle that ensued was to mark a turning point in the reign of Æthelred and in the history of England.

3
The Viking Challenge

As is the case for even momentous events during Æthelred's reign, the sources for the battle that took place near
the town of Maldon on 11 (or perhaps 10) August 991 are
problematic and details about what actually occurred are
uncertain.[1] The entry in the CDE version of the *Anglo-
Saxon Chronicle* is laconic:

> Here Ipswich was raided, and very soon after that Ealdor-
> man Byrhtnoth was killed at Maldon, and in that year it
> was decided tribute [*gafol*] be paid to the Danish men
> because of the great terror which they wrought along the
> sea coast. The first payment was ten thousand pounds.
> Archbishop Sigeric first advised this policy.[2]

The A version of the *Chronicle*, which is independent of
CDE, adds that the fleet consisted of ninety-three ships,
first landed at Folkestone in Kent, and was led by one
'Unlaf', presumably Olaf Tryggvason, the future King of
Norway, who three years later would enter into a peace
treaty with King Æthelred. This would be valuable information if reliable. Unfortunately, manuscript A misdates
the battle to 993, and, to add to the confusion, the entry

continues with events that according to CDE occurred in 994. CDE also records an unsuccessful attack on London in 994 by a fleet of ninety-four ships commanded by Olaf and Swein, the latter probably the Danish king, Swein Forkbeard.[3] There is some reason for believing that Swein Forkbeard was among the viking leaders at Maldon, and that Olaf, if present, was not in command.[4]

From reading the *Chronicle* one might get the impression that this was a single, unitary naval force. It was not. All viking fleets that were to ravage England for the next twenty-five years – even the invasion forces of King Swein and Cnut – were composite forces, made up of individual companies (termed *lith*s), recruited and commanded by Scandinavian nobles, united by the common goal of acquiring wealth.[5] The crews of these 'Danish' raiding armies were recruited from across the Scandinavian world and beyond.[6] 'Viking' is sometimes mistakenly used as a synonym for 'Scandinavian', which is why it is usually capitalized. On Scandinavian runestones and in skaldic poetry of the late tenth and early eleventh centuries, the term 'viking' in its masculine form (*víkingr*) connoted a person and in its feminine form (*víking*) the activity in which a 'viking' participated – an overseas expedition, primarily military in nature, to acquire wealth.[7] Unsurprisingly, 'viking' was a pejorative term in the writings of those whom they targeted. Archbishop Wulfstan in his 'Sermon of the Wolf' expressed particular contempt for English slaves who gained their freedom by joining viking crews. The Latin word most often used by ninth- and tenth-century English and Frankish writers to gloss 'viking' was *pirata*. Yet even 'pirate' is misleading. Vikings were, to be sure, seamen, another term often applied to them. But their targets were not vulnerable merchant ships but towns and monasteries. Ships carried vikings to their destinations. Once they arrived, they made base, secured their ships and, seizing horses, rode inland in search of plunder. The Chronicler consistently uses the Old English word *here* for viking forces, derived from the verb *hergian*, 'to harry'.

The Battle of Maldon is best remembered today because of the eponymous Old English poem it inspired that celebrates the tragic heroism of Ealdorman Byrhtnoth and his household retainers. The poem is literature, however, not history. As such it provides a window on the mentality and values of its audience. Loyalty is lauded, betrayal and failure to fulfil one's duty condemned. Byrhtnoth is presented as the ideal military leader, one who not only positions his men for battle, and rouses them with a battlefield oration, but who, despite his advanced age – and the historical ealdorman must have been at least in his early sixties[8] – stands and fights bravely. In short, the poet presents Maldon as a sort of English Thermopylae, a military defeat but a moral victory.

According to the poem, the battle occurred along the banks of the River Blackwater, near the borough of Maldon, probably at a causeway and tidal ford over the Blackwater estuary leading to Northey Island, where the vikings had landed. Whether moved by excessive pride (*ofermod*), as the poet claimed, or not, Byrhtnoth would have had a compelling practical reason for acceding to the vikings' request to allow them to cross the causeway.[9] The ealdorman's defensive position at the beginning of the battle may have been strong, but the lack of a fleet limited his strategic options.[10] Byrhtnoth could contain the vikings on their tidal island, but he could not force them to engage on his terms or prevent them from evacuating by ship. The viking fleet had already pillaged the town of Ipswich. Byrhtnoth's scouts presumably warned him about the imminent attack on Maldon, and he arrived on the scene in time to prevent the vikings from sacking the town and pillaging the surrounding countryside (where he himself appears to have held land). But to end the threat of further raids, he needed to engage and defeat the viking band, or at least inflict severe enough damage to force their withdrawal from England. In short, Byrhtnoth's strategy had to be one of annihilation. By deploying his troops on the western bank of the Blackwater, the ealdorman had stalemated rather than checkmated the enemy; only by sacrificing his impregnable position could he bring the viking raiders to battle. He had a reasonable expectation of victory. There is no indication in the sources that the English were at a numerical disadvantage. The only previous battle against viking raiders in living memory had occurred three years earlier at Watchet, and that had resulted in a victory.

Byrhtferth gives an account of the Battle of Maldon in his *Life of St Oswald* that is long on rhetoric and short on details. For both the *Maldon* poet and Byrhtferth, the significance of the battle was less its outcome than the death of Byrhtnoth. 'When the aforesaid leader was killed,' Byrhtferth writes, 'ealdormen and thegns, men and women, everyone of either sex, were deeply moved.'[11] Here Byrhtferth probably does not exaggerate. Based on his position in the witness lists, Byrhtnoth ranked second only to Æthelwine among Æthelred's ealdormen at the time of his death. By all accounts, he was an able administrator and a judicious royal counsellor, as well as a patron of monastic reform. Byrhtnoth had been also one of the few remaining links between Æthelred and his father Edgar's court. The manner of his death was what was most shocking. No ealdorman had fallen in battle in living memory. No English army had suffered defeat on the battlefield in four decades.[12] The true historical significance of Maldon is that the battle dramatically exposed England's military vulnerability.

When the vikings returned in 980 to begin a new age of raiding and invasion, they found a peaceful and wealthy England ripe for pillaging. It was certainly a well-administered, or at least highly administered, kingdom, in which the central government had in place mechanisms for the maintenance of internal order and the raising of revenues. But one should not mistake bureaucratic efficiency and ideological sophistication for military strength. The military system that King Alfred had created to defend Wessex and that his son, daughter and grandsons used to conquer the Danelaw had deteriorated by the time Æthelred ascended the throne. The civil defence system that Æthelred inherited relied on royal armies (termed *fyrd*s in the sources) raised by ad hoc levies of landowners and their retainers. They were summoned by royal command in the case of national efforts, and by ealdormen in defence of localities. Military service, whether on land or sea, was treated as a tax on land, with individual landowners owing and responsible for a quota of soldiers based, roughly, on the value of their property. Anglo-Saxon armies were organized by shire and hundred, and were not only ass- embled but also led by royal reeves and ealdormen. As in *The Battle of Maldon*, the professional core of the army con- sisted of the household troops of the king, ealdormen and great magnates. Maintenance of the warships of King Edgar's mighty fleet was left to local authorities, and by 991 many were no longer in serviceable condition. None of England's many towns were defended by permanent mili- tary garrisons; even those with walls were little more than places of refuge for the surrounding population. This was a military designed for peacetime, and an indicator of the country's remarkable security and stability. At least in this sense, Æthelred and his advisers were unready to meet the new viking threat.

Ealdorman Byrhtnoth's defeat at Maldon in 991 con- vinced Æthelred and his counsellors of the gravity of the situation and the wisdom of purchasing peace. The Chronic- ler blames the policy on Sigeric, Archbishop of Canterbury, and, with the benefit of hindsight, is clearly critical of the decision. He knew that this was to be but the first of many such payments, which would become increasingly heavy as the invading armies grew larger and hungrier. The £10,000 offered to the raiders in 991, however, was probably the only way to stop them from ravaging at will.

Payment of tribute was one traditional method of dealing with vikings. It had been practised by both Carolingian and English kings in the ninth century, including Alfred the

Great. The problem was that truces thus purchased were temporary. The Chronicler gives the impression that the viking fleet, termed consistently the *here* (raiding army), continued to operate in English waters for the next four years. The £10,000, however, bought time for the English to prepare militarily. The following year, Æthelred, on the advice of his counsellors, ordered 'that those ships that were worth anything' – an indication of the condition of Edgar's once formidable fleet – should be assembled in London. Rather than taking command of the fleet himself, King Æthelred entrusted it to Ealdorman Ælfric of Hampshire, Earl Thored of York, Bishop Ælfstan of Rochester and Bishop Æscwig of Dorchester, and ordered them to attempt to trap the *here* at sea or in the estuary.[13]

They failed. Indeed, the campaign was a complete fiasco. The Chronicler blames this on treachery, which was to be a leitmotif in his narrative. According to him, Ealdorman Ælfric, 'one of those in whom the king had most trust', sent advance warning to the enemy fleet and, on the night before the battle was to take place, 'scurried away from the army, to his own disgrace'.[14] When the English fleet rowed out to engage the enemy, they discovered that the viking fleet had sailed off, leaving behind only one beached ship. The ships from East Anglia and London pursued the raiders but suffered defeat when they intercepted the viking fleet. Adding to the shame, the vikings captured the ealdorman's own ship, along with its stored weapons and equipment. Ealdorman Ælfric, surprisingly, retained his office, which might indicate that the 'treachery' was not as blatant as the Chronicler makes it out to be. The disorder and confusion may have been due simply to inexperience. Given the generally peaceful conditions of Edgar's reign, this was probably the first time that any of the four co-captains had been in command of either a land or naval force. Ælfric remained the Ealdorman of Hampshire, but the debacle may have lowered him in the king's esteem. Two years later, Æthelred ordered the ealdorman's son Ælfgar to be blinded. We are not told why.[15] Earl Thored disappears from the witness lists.

This was the first time, and was not to be the last, that King Æthelred delegated command of a national army or fleet with disastrous results. Given the size of the kingdom, it made military sense that ealdormen should bear the responsibility of defending the shires under their authority, and be authorized to act autonomously. That was a primary duty of the office, although for several decades prior to Æthelred's ascension probably only ealdormen on the Welsh and Scottish frontiers would have been called upon to do so. The return of the vikings changed matters. It is probably not coincidental that Ealdorman Æthelweard's Latin rendering of the *Anglo-Saxon Chronicle* emphasizes far more than its vernacular source the military role played by ealdormen in King Alfred's defence of Wessex against the first wave of viking invaders.[16] In the 980s, local royal officials, probably mostly town- or shire-reeves, responded to small-scale raiding. Because of the size of the viking fleet, Ealdorman Byrhtnoth led the Essex levy, probably augmented with forces raised from the south-east Midland counties that belonged to his ealdormanry, in defence of the town of Maldon and its surrounding areas. The viking threat was still at this point seen as a local matter to be dealt with by regional officers of the crown.

The English fleet assembled in the wake of the Battle of Maldon in 991, however, was a national force. Based on the actions of his predecessors, Æthelred, then a young man in his early-to-mid twenties, would have been expected to command the fleet in person. Instead he delegated the responsibility. We are not told why, but Æthelred was to follow this policy throughout his reign. Only three times did he lead an army on campaign. In 1000 he commanded a combined land and sea force in a ravaging expedition directed against Cumberland and the Isle of Man. Nine years later, Æthelred was at the head of an army that stood between Thorkell the Tall's viking army and its ships, but on the advice of Ealdorman Eadric Streona thought it best not to engage. Upon his return from exile in Normandy in 1014, Æthelred conducted his third and final campaign, a ravaging expedition to Lindsey (what is now northern Lincolnshire) to punish the shire for having given its support to Cnut. On several other occasions, he was with armies or fleets that failed for one reason or another to engage the enemy. Æthelred came from a long line of warrior-kings; he himself was not one. He and his advisers may have been sensitive to appearances, however. If Æthelred did not show himself to be a warrior-king in the field, he could represent himself as one on his coins. The 'Helmet' penny, issued about the time of Swein's return to England in 1003, depicts a helmeted Æthelred in Roman armour, a martial image based upon a fourth-century imperial coin.[17] One can only imagine the reactions of Swein and Æthelred's military commanders on seeing the king decked out like this.

To judge from a letter, 'Wyrdwriteras' (Historians), written by the homilist Ælfric, Æthelred's reluctance to lead armies attracted criticism and perhaps even suspicions of cowardice. In this text, Ælfric responds to those critics by citing historical precedents for Æthelred's policy of delegating military command. In the writings of Roman historians and the Bible, he observes, there are numerous examples of kings who enjoyed military success by entrusting their armies to generals. Ælfric commends that practice as prudent. The life of a king, he asserts, is too important to risk in battle, and royal responsibilities too great for a king to be preoccupied with warfare.[18] Even if sanctioned by scripture, Ælfric's argument was a radical reconceptualization of the king's role in war. It flew in the face of what was expected of a monarch. Everyone, including Æthelred, acknowledged that the presence or absence of a king on campaign mattered. Æthelred's own laws make this clear. The penalty for deserting an army led by the king was either death or the confiscation of the offender's property. In contrast, a deserter of an army led by anyone else faced a fine of just 120 shillings.[19]

One should not underestimate the symbolic and emotional weight placed on the king's person. Political allegiance in the tenth century was a species of personal loyalty, with kingship regarded as the highest form of lordship.[20] Although the king is not present in body in the poem *The Battle of Maldon*, he is in spirit, as the poet describes Byrhtnoth variously as 'Æthelred's thegn' (line 151) and 'Æthelred's earl' (line 203). The earl dies defending the

45

'kingdom of Æthelred, my lord's people and his country' (lines 52–4).[21] The itineration of the royal court among the king's estates and the various locales in which the witan met brought landowners directly into the king's presence, reinforcing the pledges of loyalty they had given in their local hundreds.[22]

Loyalty to the person of the king was the glue that unified an English kingdom so recently forged from separate peoples. The ætheling Edmund would discover this at the very end of his father's reign in 1016, when he attempted to assemble on his own a national army to oppose Cnut. The army dissolved when its leaders discovered that Æthelred was not in the camp. According to John of Worcester (d. c.1140), in the absence of the king 'the Mercians would not engage with the West Saxons and Danes'.[23] Nor should one ignore the practical military value of a leader, such as Byrhtnoth at Maldon (or, for that matter, the aged Beowulf in the eponymous epic poem), demonstrating and modelling the prowess and courage he expected from his followers. Morale and discipline were essential ingredients for the success of a shield wall, and the presence of one's lord fighting in the front ranks at the risk of his own life increased the likelihood that his men would stand and fight. As one of the sayings in the *Durham Proverbs* puts it: 'The entire army is whatever its leader is.'[24] And if a commander proved irresolute, it was expected that his troops would be as well. The maxim quoted by the *Anglo-Saxon Chronicle*'s entry for 1003 – 'When the commander weakens, the whole army is greatly hindered'[25] – is at least as old as the eighth-century scholar Alcuin, who gives a variation on it in his letter to Eanbald, Archbishop of York: 'If he who bears the standard flees, what does the army do? . . . If the leader is fearful, how shall the soldier be saved?'[26]

The Chronicler might have responded to Ælfric that the generals whom he cited were not only successful but served their kings loyally, whereas Æthelred's were neither, and Ælfric would have agreed. The Chronicler explicitly and Ælfric implicitly criticize Æthelred for showing poor judgement in his choice of advisers and generals. The Chronicler's account of the viking wars is a rather monotonous litany of treachery and betrayal. He attributes the military failures of the English in both 992 and 993 to the treachery or cowardice of the leaders of the English forces. In 992 the cause had been the desertion of Ealdorman Ælfric. The following year, when a large army was raised against the vikings in the north, the English again lost because their leaders, Godwine, Fræna and Frithugist, 'set the example of flight'.[27] Ealdorman Ælfric, we are assured by the Chronicler, betrayed Æthelred's trust once again in 1003, when, 'up to his old tricks', he feigned illness, allowing Swein Forkbeard to sack and burn the town of Wilton and ravage the countryside at will. The poster boy for treachery, Eadric Streona, Ealdorman of Mercia from 1007 to 1017, betrayed both Æthelred and his son King Edmund 'Ironside' several times, for which Cnut rewarded him by retaining him as Earl of Mercia. Within a year, however, the Danish king had a change of heart and ordered that Eadric be executed, 'so that soldiers may learn from this example to be faithful, not faithless, to their kings'.[28]

For the Chronicler and other Anglo-Saxon authors such

as the *Maldon* poet, cowardice, treachery and failure to do the duty owed a lord were indistinguishable.[29] But one must be careful about accepting uncritically the Chronicler's accusations. Ælfric, whom Æthelred (or his regents) appointed ealdorman in 982, retained his office until his death in 1016 fighting for Æthelred's son King Edmund Ironside in the Battle of Assandun. Godwine, the son of Ealdorman Ælfheah of Hampshire, reappears in the *Anglo-Saxon Chronicle* in 1016 as Ealdorman of Lindsey, while the thegns Fræna of Rockingham and Frithugist, son of Cate, appear in charters as benefactors of Peterborough Abbey. The former, an important landowner in the Danelaw and a member of Æthelred's court, attested royal charters with some regularity between 994 and 1004.[30] It would have been odd that men accused of treachery in 992 and 993 would have continued to hold land and royal offices years later. It is more likely that the Chronicler, looking for a morally satisfying explanation for the English defeat, interpreted the military failures and errors by Æthelred's commanders as acts of treachery. Some undoubtedly were, or, at least, Æthelred believed them to be, and the men he thought to be traitors were punished by death, blinding or, if the accused was fortunate, exile.

Between 991 and 994, Æthelred and his advisers alternated between paying tribute and at least attempting to fight the viking raiders, who apparently continued to operate in English waters without interruption. By 993 the *here* was a composite fleet of ninety-four ships under the command of several captains, the most prominent being Olaf Tryggvason, a Norwegian adventurer who claimed to be of royal blood, and Swein Forkbeard, King of Denmark. The two were anything but natural allies. Like so many other viking warlords in the ninth and tenth centuries, Olaf was a would-be king who went a-viking to obtain the wealth and support necessary to realize his ambitions at home. His goal was to take the throne of Norway, which placed him at odds with Swein, as Danish kings had long regarded Norway as a tributary state.[31] King Swein's reasons for conducting viking raids also arose from the political situation in Scandinavia. In 993 Swein's hold on the Danish throne was probably secure. But the kingdom that he had wrested from his father, Harald Bluetooth, was no longer as dominant a power in Scandinavia as it had once been. Towards the end of Harald's reign, the rulers of both Norway and Sweden had repudiated his lordship. England offered Swein the wealth and prestige he needed to return them to the status of tributary rulers.

Swein's and Olaf's ambitions were in direct conflict. What brought the Danish king and the Norse adventurer together was their common goal of plundering the riches of England, and they had been fabulously successful in this endeavour. This culminated in September 993 with an attack on the largest city in England, London.[32] London was also the most well-defended town in England and withstood the first of several sieges it would undergo during the viking wars. The Chronicler, who may have been a Londoner, comments proudly that the vikings wished to set the city on fire but 'suffered more harm and injury than they ever imagined that any burgesses would do to them', which he attributes to the mercy of 'the holy Mother of God'. Olaf and Swein broke off the siege and turned first to ravaging along the coasts of Kent, Sussex and Hampshire, followed by riding inland and 'wreaking indescribable harm' as widely as they could. On the advice of Archbishop Sigeric, Ealdorman Ælfric and Ealdorman Æthelweard, King Æthelred offered to pay them £16,000 and provide them with supplies to desist.[33] Viking leaders always welcomed the prospect of a negotiated 'peace'. Not only was it a less risky way to acquire wealth, but, just as importantly, it was the surest means of securing provisions. With winter looming, the prospect of having the English providing food and drink rather than having to forage for them was appealing to the several thousand men who made up the viking *here*. The Scandinavian fleet took up winter quarters at Southampton while the English officials raised the tribute money and gathered food from throughout the country to feed them.

Seeing an opportunity to divide his enemies, King Æthelred sent Bishop Ælfheah of Winchester and Ealdorman Æthelweard to Southampton to invite Olaf to meet with him at the royal palace of Andover, thirty miles to the north.[34] As a sign of good faith, the king sent hostages to the fleet to guarantee Olaf's safety. The bishop and ealdorman then conducted Olaf to Andover 'with great honour'.[35] Although the Chronicler does not mention them, Olaf was accompanied by two lesser Scandinavian captains, Jostein and Guthmund. Conspicuous by his absence is Swein. Æthelred's intention went beyond securing a cessation of hostilities. The £16,000 and supplies that he had given to the *here* wintering at Southampton had done that much. Æthelred's ultimate goal was to transform this *here* into a force that could be used to deter and oppose other viking armies. The £22,000 Æthelred paid the three viking leaders was for a general peace (*woroldfrið*) rather than a mere truce. The treaty Æthelred negotiated with the viking leaders at Andover stipulated that

(1.1). If any hostile fleet harry in England, we are to have the help of all of them; and we must supply them with provisions as long as they are with us.

(1.2). And each of those lands which affords protection to any of those who harry England shall be regarded as an enemy by us and by the whole *here*.[36]

As the Danish historian Niels Lund observes, *II Æthelred*, as it is called, reads more like a contractual agreement of employment for mercenary troops than a peace treaty.[37] Those who accepted the peace were to defend England against future raiders and aid Æthelred against foreign rulers who harboured them. Because viking leaders and their crews were to reside among the English, the treaty prohibits anyone from seeking vengeance or compensation from them for 'the slaughter and all the harrying and all injuries committed before the truce was established'.[38] Æthelred endowed some of the fleet's leaders, most notably a Dane named Pallig, with estates in return for a pledge of loyalty, in an attempt to embed them into existing political and social structures.[39] Others were housed as military units in towns.

Æthelred marked out Olaf for special treatment. He sought a more personal relationship with the ambitious viking adventurer, preferably one in which he would be the

superior. The instrument he chose was one employed by ear-
lier Anglo-Saxon and Carolingian kings, Christian spiritual
kinship. Olaf apparently had been previously baptized. At
Andover, Æthelred stood sponsor at his confirmation by
Bishop Ælfheah; by doing so, he transformed an enemy into
a spiritual son.[40] The transaction was consummated by
Æthelred, in his role as gift-giving lord, bestowing upon
Olaf gifts befitting a king. Olaf, however, did not become
Æthelred's mercenary captain, a role that another viking
chieftain, Thorkell the Tall, would play in the last years of
his reign. But he did the next best thing. Enriched with English treasure and accompanied by English missionaries,
Olaf returned to Norway to seize the kingship in defiance of
Swein's claims over that kingdom.[41] For once the Chronicler
approves: 'And then Olaf promised – as also he performed –
that he would never come back to England in hostility.'[42]
Æthelred got more from this than simply the removal of one
viking chieftain. As he and his advisers hoped, Olaf's return
to Norway created domestic problems for Swein of Denmark. After a popular uprising had disposed of the de facto
ruler of Norway, King Harald Bluetooth's erstwhile client
Earl Håkon Sigurdsson, the Norwegians took Olaf as their
king. Swein followed Olaf back to Scandinavia, and formed
a coalition against him with his stepson King Olof Sköt-
konung of Sweden and Earl Håkon's son Erik. Five years
later, Erik, with Danish and Swedish support, avenged his
father by ambushing and killing Olaf as he returned from a
campaign in Pomerania in the Battle of Svold.

As Æthelred and his advisers foresaw when they made
peace with Olaf, Jostein and Guthmund, it was only a matter

of time before other *here*s would come, lured by the prospect of wealth. In 997 a viking fleet ravaged Wales and the south-western shires of England. Rather than oppose them, some of Æthelred's new Danish mercenaries succumbed to the temptation of easy loot and returned to their old ways. Over the next two years, this viking fleet raided along the coast of southern England from Cornwall to Kent. The failure of local forces to end the marauding persuaded Æthelred and his advisers of the necessity of a national response. The king ordered that both a land-*fyrd* and a ship-*fyrd* be assembled. The Chronicler claims that in the end this achieved nothing 'except wasting the people's labour and money, and embold-ening of their enemies'.[43] The waste of time, labour and money due to incompetence and treachery is a theme that runs throughout the Chronicler's narrative of the viking wars. But here, at least, one may question the accuracy of his assessment. In the summer of 1000, the viking fleet left Eng-land for Normandy without the inducement of tribute.

Æthelred took advantage of the departure of the vikings to launch a land and sea campaign in 1000 against the kingdom of Strathclyde (Cumberland) and the Isle of Man. The sources do not explain why, but it might have been precipitated by a resurgence of Hiberno-Norse viking activity in the Irish Sea following King Brian Boru's expulsion of the Norse from Dublin in 999, or by the threat of a Scottish invasion. The campaign also announced to neighbouring British kings that Æthelred had not abandoned his father Edgar's imperial claims to be 'ruler of the whole of Britain'.[44] Perhaps that is why Æthelred atypically took personal command of the exp-edition. The army led by Æthelred harried Strathclyde, and the

English fleet, which failed to rendezvous with the land forces as planned, ravaged the Isle of Man. The respite from viking raids was brief. A large viking fleet returned to England the following year, ravaging Hampshire, Devonshire and the Isle of Wight. The Hampshire levies engaged them at Æthelingadene (Dean, Sussex). Although the Danes won the battle, they suffered heavier losses than the English. The casualties of the English numbered eighty-six, which included two high-reeves and two king's thegns, a figure that puts into perspective what the Chronicler meant by a 'great slaughter'.[45] The vikings continued west to Devon, where they were joined by Pallig, one of Æthelred's Danish mercenary captains, 'with those ships he could gather'.[46] Despite receiving a payment of tribute, the viking army continued to ravage Devonshire. The Devonshire *fyrd* led by the king's high-reeve met the vikings at Pinhoe but was put to flight. After pillaging and burning estates in Devonshire, the viking army ravaged the Isle of Wight before making winter camp there.

Unable to dislodge them from their base, Æthelred and his advisers decided to pay tribute. In return for ceasing their 'evil-doing', the English agreed to pay the viking army £24,000 and supply them with provisions.[47] Once again, tribute bought a respite from viking attacks, which Æthelred used to take preventive counter-measures. A standing problem was the aid that vikings had been receiving from Duke Richard II of Normandy in violation of a treaty that Æthelred had made with the duke's father. A decade earlier, Duke Richard I, himself the descendant of vikings, had allowed Norman ports to be used as staging grounds for piratical raids on England. By 991 tensions between

Æthelred and the Norman duke had become serious enough to warrant papal intervention.[48] A papal legate brokered a peace treaty between the king and the duke that featured a promise not to give refuge to each other's enemies. The 'unshaken peace' created by this treaty apparently lapsed with the death of Duke Richard I in 996. The surest way to close the ports of Normandy to vikings was to establish a strong personal tie with his son, Duke Richard II. This was done through a marriage alliance. In 1002 Æthelred took the duke's sister Emma as his wife. (The fate of Æthelred's shadowy first wife and mother of his first eight children is unknown.) Perhaps in consequence of negotiations between Æthelred and Duke Richard II, Emma was consecrated queen at the time of the marriage.[49] She was also given the English name Ælfgifu, after her husband's sainted grandmother. In her second marriage, to Cnut in 1017, after the death of Æthelred, Emma-Ælgifu was to emerge as a more potent political force than even Ælfthryth had been.

There would be no rivalry between these two formidable women. The dowager queen had passed away in either the spring of 1001 or 1000.[50] In 1002 Æthelred issued a charter 'for the care of the souls of my father Edgar and my mother Ælfthryth', confirming the lands of the nunnery that his mother founded at Wherwell, Hampshire, and to which she may have retired in her waning years.[51] To this the king added his mother's estate at Æthelingadene, the site of the battle of the previous year. In conformity with the *Regularis Concordia*, he also granted the nunnery the privilege of free elections in consultation with the bishop.[52]

He honoured Wherwell further with an oblation of one of his daughters, who subsequently became its abbess. As Levi Roach notes, the proem to the charter concludes suggestively with a quotation from the Bible: 'Honor your father and mother that you may be long lived upon the land.'[53]

Æthelred took advantage of the lull in viking attacks to correct what he now saw as a miscalculation. Not only had the Danish mercenaries failed to defend his lands as they had pledged to do, they had joined with his enemies. Particularly infuriating were the actions of the Danish jarl Pallig. Contrary to all the pledges he had given and despite the estates and gold and silver that Æthelred had bestowed upon him, Pallig deserted the service of Æthelred and reverted to his viking ways. He gathered together as many ships as he could from the Danes in Æthelred's employ, and met the viking fleet as it arrived in Devon. But instead of fighting the raiders, as he was obliged by the treaty and their oaths, Pallig and his followers joined the vikings in pillaging Devon.[54] In early November 1002, Æthelred was told of a plot by Danes dwelling in England to kill him and all his counsellors. The king's response was the so-called 'Saint Brice's Day Massacre', undoubtedly the darkest stain on his posthumous reputation. Æthelred ordered that 'all the Danish men who were among the English race be killed on Brice's Day' (13 November).[55] That something along these lines was actually carried out is attested by a charter issued by Æthelred two years later to the monastery of St Frideswide in Oxford. The king granted to the monks a new privilege for their lands because the old deeds had been lost when the townspeople burned the church during a massacre of Danes:

To all dwelling in this country it will be well known that, since a decree was sent out by me with the counsel of my leading men and magnates, to the effect that all the Danes who had sprung up in this island, sprouting like cockle [wild wheat] amongst the wheat [Matthew 13:25], were to be destroyed by a most just extermination, and this decree was to be put into effect even as far as death, those Danes who dwelt in the afore-mentioned town, striving to escape death, entered this sanctuary of Christ, having broken by force the doors and bolts, and resolved to make a refuge and defence for themselves therein against the people of the town and the suburbs; but when all the people in pursuit strove, forced by necessity, to drive them out, and could not, they set fire to the planks and burnt, as it seems, this church with its ornaments and its books.[56]

The charter's allusion to the biblical parable of the cockle among the wheat can be read as justifying not only the royal edict itself but also the extreme manner in which it had been carried out in Oxford, as the parable instructs that the invasive weeds should be gathered together and burned. By likening the Danes to the cockle of the parable, the king signalled his approval of what was an egregious violation of the 'peace of the church'.[57] That the townspeople of Oxford had been willing to burn down a church in order to kill their Danish neighbours who had sought – and probably expected – to find sanctuary there is an indication of the intense anger and hatred engendered by more than a decade of viking depredation. The Danes of Oxford were clearly a people apart.

It is difficult to read this charter and not think of

modern-day ethnic cleansing. Certainly, that is what Norman and Anglo-Norman historians beginning with William of Jumièges around 1060 believed it to be. Paralleling their account of Queen Ælfthryth, these writers describe in ever more horrendous detail the brutal and pitiless slaying of defenceless women and children.[58] But, as with all the sources for this period, the St Frideswide's charter cannot be taken at face value. Æthelred's edict could not have been sent to 'all dwelling in this country'. There were no massacres in the Danelaw or even evidence of tensions between inhabitants of Danish and English descent, if such a distinction even made sense in 1002. Men with Scandinavian names continued to frequent Æthelred's court. The crucial question is who were the 'cockle' in Oxford? In 2008 archaeologists uncovered in the grounds of St John's College, Oxford, a mass burial containing the skeletons of a minimum of thirty-six males. With the exception of two twelve- or fourteen-year-old boys, these men ranged in age from sixteen to forty-five, with the majority in their twenties. They had all died violent deaths: the skulls of twenty-seven had been broken, and all had been repeatedly stabbed. Some had healed scars from earlier wounds, as might be expected of viking raiders or mercenaries. Significantly, in light of the St Frideswide's charter, about a third had charred bones. Radiocarbon and isotopic analyses have dated the bones to between 960 and 1025 and identified the men as being of Scandinavian origin. If these were victims of the Saint Brice's Day Massacre, as seems likely, the killing in Oxford had not been indiscriminate but was targeted against males of military age, mercenaries residing in the town.[59] The

Saint Brice's Day Massacre is therefore best understood as Æthelred's solution to the mercenary problem.[60]

The following year Swein resumed his raiding of England. By the 1060s, stories circulated that had Swein returning to exact vengeance for the massacre. According to both the Norman historian William of Jumièges and his contemporary the German chronicler Adam of Bremen, the Danish magnates demanded that Swein avenge the murders of their friends and kinsmen. The twelfth-century chronicler William of Malmesbury makes Swein's motivation more personal, explaining that he was avenging the deaths of his sister Gunnhild and her husband Pallig, but his account is chronologically muddled and there is no evidence that Swein even had a sister by that name or that Pallig and his wife were victims of the massacre.[61] It is possible that Swein had heard reports of the killings, but if they were directed against mercenaries in Æthelred's employment, he might not have been all that upset by the news. It is more likely that his return was a consequence of his having successfully re-established Danish hegemony within Scandinavia.

Over the next two years, Swein raided throughout southern England. The Chronicler, always on the lookout for traitors, incompetents and cowards, blames the burning of Exeter on the town-reeve, a French commoner (*ceorl*) whom the new Norman queen had appointed. The burning of Wilton, according to the Chronicler, was the fault of Ealdorman Ælfric, who feigned illness to avoid engaging Swein with the shire forces of Hampshire and Wiltshire. More atypically, the Chronicler praises the heroism of Ulfcytel of East Anglia, a king's thegn who seems to have fulfilled the duties of ealdorman without the title. In 1004 the Danes sacked and burned the town of Norwich, which led Ulf- cytel and the witan of East Anglia to attempt to negotiate a peace. After the Danes violated the peace and Ulfcytel's plan to destroy their ships failed, Ulfcytel raised as large a force as he could on short notice to intercept the Danes as they returned to their ships laden with booty from Thet- ford. The Chronicler for once approves of the efforts of an English military leader. He excuses the decision of Ulfcytel and his counsellors to pay tribute by saying that the raiders had come so unexpectedly that they had had no time to raise an army. Although the English lost the battle, in which many of the leading men of East Anglia fell, the Chronicler praises the bravery of the outnumbered East Anglians, adding that the Danes themselves admitted that they would never have made it back to the ships if the English had been at full strength and that 'they had never met with harder hand-play in England than Ulfcytel gave them'.[62] One may see in this the influence of a now lost poem much like that of the Battle of Maldon.

Where Ulfcytel's courage and resolution failed, famine succeeded. In 1005 England suffered a famine 'such that no one ever remembered one so grim before'. The viking fleet sailed back to Denmark, although the Chronicler bitterly notes that they would soon return.[63]

4
The Politics of Repentance

When Æthelred ordered the Saint Brice's Day Massacre in 1002, he was no longer a boy-king. The massacre was not an action taken out of 'youthful ignorance' but a considered decision made with the advice and consent of the leading men of the realm. As the St Frideswide charter's allusion to the parable of the cockle among the wheat suggests, the 'most just extermination' was to be seen as springing from the righteous anger of a Christian king against those who endangered his kingdom. Æthelred's transformation from impetuous youth to mature ruler had taken place a decade earlier. As can be seen from his charters, the early 990s represent a turning point in Æthelred's reign, the transition from what Simon Keynes has termed 'the period of youthful indiscretions' to 'the years of maturity'.[1]

The change is most visible in the composition of Æthelred's witan and court. The deaths of Archbishop Dunstan of Canterbury in 988 and Ealdorman Byrhtnoth of Essex in 991, and of Archbishop Oswald of York, Ealdorman Æthelwine of East Anglia and possibly Æthelred's father-in-law Earl Thored the following year, deprived the king of his most senior advisers. The leading ealdormen were now Æthelweard in the south-west and Ælfric of Hampshire, who weathered the fiasco of 992. They were also the only ealdor-men south of the Thames. Æthelred immediately selected replacements for Byrhtnoth and Thored, choosing in the lat-ter case a Mercian rather than a member of one of the two Northumbrian families that had traditionally held that office. Mercia had been without an ealdorman since the exile of Ælfric *cild* in 985. In 994 Æthelred partially remed-ied that by appointing an ealdorman for western Mercia (Worcestershire, Gloucestershire and Warwickshire). The family of Æthelstan Half King's hold over East Anglia came to an end with the death of Æthelwine. Æthelred left the ealdormanry unfilled, entrusting some of the responsibil-ities of the office, most critically defence of the region, to a prominent local thegn, Ulfcytel 'of the East Angles', who, as we have seen, exercised those duties admirably.

Whole regions of England were left without an ealdorman. This does not mean, however, that they were without royal government. The absence of an ealdorman simply meant that a high-reeve answered directly to the king rather than through an intermediary. Based on their prominence in charter wit-ness lists of the 990s, Æthelred relied particularly on the counsel of three of his kinsmen: his maternal uncle Ordulf; Æthelmær, the son of Ealdorman Æthelweard; and Briht-wold. A group of new names also appears among the *ministri*, the thegns of the king's court, men who in some cases would remain prominent throughout the remainder of Æthelred's reign. Perhaps most significantly, Queen Ælfthryth is once again found attesting her son's charters as 'the king's mother'. Æthelred demonstrated his restored confidence in her by entrusting his eldest son, Æthelstan, to her care.[2]

As some rose, others fell. This was particularly true for the men who had formed Æthelred's inner circle of advisers and household officers in the mid 880s. By 993, Æthelred had come to regret his willingness to allow these favourites to prey upon church lands. Ultimately, as king he bore the responsibility, but kings, especially young and inexperienced ones, rely upon advisers to guide them. Looking back, Æthelred came to the conclusion that those to whom he had given his trust had led him astray. Five prominent king's thegns in the charters of the 980s disappear between 990 and 995: the royal seneschals (*disciferi*) Ælfweard and Ælfsige, whose services stretched back to Edgar's reign; Wulfsige; Ælfgar, probably the son of Ealdorman Ælfric, whom Æthelred ordered to be blinded in 993; and Æthelsige, who was deprived of lands and office for having killed a king's reeve. The last two were among those whom the king had allowed to despoil church lands. As we have seen, Ælfgar had appropriated estates belonging to both the Old Minster and Abingdon, while the granting to Æthelsige by Æthelred of the estate of Bromley in Kent had led to the king's ravaging of the diocese of Rochester, the act of his youth that that he most regretted.[3] Ten years later, he repented both the act and his support of a man who (in the words of a charter) had proved to be an 'enemy of God almighty and the whole people' by killing a royal reeve who tried to interfere with his many acts of theft and plunder.[4]

No charters survive for the years 991 and 992, arguably a consequence of the disruptive impact of Olaf and Swein's attacks upon the ordinary processes of English government during these years. This silence was broken in 993 with a remarkable diploma, a confirmation of privileges to Abingdon Abbey, which may provide one of the few windows that historians have into Æthelred's inner self.[5] In its narrative section, the charter relates how the king, meditating upon the many afflictions and perils his country had suffered following the death of his 'most dear Bishop Æthelwold', looked inward and concluded that the cause was wrongdoings he had committed 'partly on account of the ignorance of my youth . . . and partly on account of the abhorrent greed of those men who ought to administer to my interest'.[6] He especially regretted his treatment of the abbey of Abingdon, in which he had accepted money for recognizing Ealdorman Ælfric's brother Eadwine as its abbot, disregarding the privilege of free election that his predecessors had granted the abbey. Desiring absolution from the terrifying anathemas he had incurred and in consultation with Abbot Ælfsige of the New Minster, Abbot Wulfgar of Abingdon, whom he had appointed in 990, and his kinsmen Ordulf and Æthelmær, the king summoned a synodal council at Winchester where, in the presence of his bishops, abbots and ealdormen, he expressed remorse and pledged to restore to Abingdon its liberty and the lands that perfidious men had unjustly appropriated with his consent. He did this, he added, not for money but rather for the freely given prayers and masses chanted on his behalf by the monks. Six weeks later, at a meeting held in Gillingham, Æthelred formally issued the charter making good on his promises. Fittingly, given her friendship with Bishop Æthelwold, among those witnessing this charter was Ælfthryth, who attests as 'the king's mother'.

She appears immediately after the bishops and before her grandsons Æthelstan and Eogbert.

This was the first of several charters in which Æthelred expressed remorse and made restitution to Abingdon, the Old Minster, Winchester, and St Andrew's, Rochester.[7] Especially expressive is a charter of 998, written as if in the king's own words, by which Æthelred made restoration to the cathedral church of Rochester and estate in Kent after being misled by the unscrupulous Æthelsige into ravaging the diocese:

> Now, however, since I have reached the age of understanding I have determined to correct for the better what I performed childishly ... Now I completely repent with a tearful contrition of the heart before God, and I freely restore whatever belonging to the same place is fitting, hoping that the tears of my repentance will be accepted and that the chains of my earlier ignorance will be shattered by Him who does not wish the death of the sinner but rather that he might turn back and live.[8]

As Catherine Cubitt has pointed out, this is the language of penance. She argues that Æthelred in 993 adopted a 'penitential style of kingship' that had long been employed by Carolingian and Ottonian kings. It allowed Æthelred to repudiate past actions and to begin his reign anew as a pious and virtuous ruler.[9] Levi Roach goes further. He hears the king's own voice in these charters. For him, Æthelred was not simply adopting the symbolic penitential language as a political strategy to enhance his kingship but was expressing true remorse.[10] Both views, of course, may be right.

Whether the words of the charters were those of Æthelred or a scribe, there is no reason to doubt that they reflected the king's own thoughts and concerns.

Æthelred's remorse was expressed not only in his restitution of lands to despoiled monasteries but in the individuals he now chose as his advisers. Most of the men he selected to be bishops had been trained by either Archbishop Dunstan or Bishop Æthelwold. Their career paths had typically taken them from the monastery to the episcopacy. This was true of Dunstan's successors in the archiepiscopal see of Canterbury: Æthelgar (988–90); Sigeric (990–94); (Saint) Ælfric (995–1005); and (Saint) Ælfheah (1006–12). Wulfstan, who in his dual capacity as Archbishop of York (1002–23) and Bishop of Worcester (1002–16) was to be the foremost churchman in the courts of both Æthelred and Cnut, makes his first appearance in the historical record in 996 with his appointment as Bishop of London. Although Wulfstan's earlier career is obscure, from his corpus of writings it is almost certain that he too had been a monk. All these men were strong supporters of Benedictine monasticism. This was the case as well for several of the most prominent laymen who frequented Æthelred's court. Wulfric Spot, whose brother Ælfhelm was ealdorman of southern Northumbria, was a generous patron of Burton Abbey, and may have had a hand in its refoundation. Ealdorman Æthelweard's son Æthelmær the Stout founded or refounded the abbeys of Cerne Abbas (987) and Eynsham (1005). He, like his father, was a patron of the homilist Ælfric, who dedicated to him his *Lives of the Saints*. The king's uncle Ordulf was the founder of Tavistock Abbey. Ordulf and Æthelmær, along with Wulfgeat,

1. Pharaoh has his chief baker hanged in a depiction of an Anglo-Saxon king with his witan from the Old English Hexateuch, second quarter of the eleventh century.

2. A view of the causeway to Northey Island, Essex, the likely site of the Battle of Maldon in August 991.

3. The Sea Stallion from Glendalough, a modern reconstruction of the great longship Skuldelev 2. Discovered in Roskilde Fjord, Denmark, in 1957, it is typical of the vessels that the vikings would have used in their devastating raids on England during Æthelred's reign.

4. Reconstruction of the small viking longship Skuldelev 5.

5. The Orkesta runestone U 344, one of about thirty runestones, most of them in Sweden, that refer to viking raids on England. The inscription commemorates the payments that the viking Ulf received from Tosti in 1006, Thorkell the Tall in 1012 and Cnut in 1018 on expeditions to England.

6. Restitution of lands and liberties to Abingdon Abbey, 993, recorded in the first of several charters in which Æthelred expressed remorse for the wrongful appropriation of church lands by favourites who took advantage of his 'youthful ignorance'.

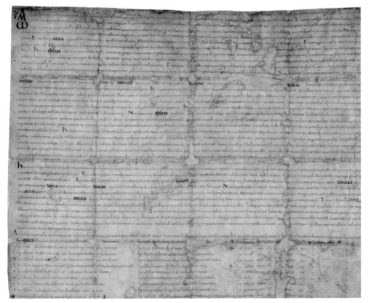

7. A silver 'Helmet' penny, minted in London, *c*.1003. The obverse shows the king in profile and the reverse a Christian cross. The coin, issued around the time of King Swein's renewed raids on England, represents Æthelred as a martial Roman emperor.

8. A silver penny of Æthelred, Agnus Dei type, minted in Derby in 1009. It was issued in conjunction with a programme of national penance after the failure of the armada assembled the previous year. The king's portrait is absent: the obverse features the Lamb of God and the reverse a dove, symbol of the Holy Spirit.

9. Cissbury Ring, Wilton, one of the 'emergency' boroughs King Æthelred ordered to be built on top of reoccupied Iron Age hill forts to protect royal mints from viking raiders.

10. Old Sarum, ancient Salisbury, in Wiltshire – another of King Æthelred's 'emergency' boroughs.

11. Possible victims of the Saint Brice's Day Massacre ordered by Æthelred on 13 November 1002, in a mass grave excavated at St John's College, Oxford, in 2008.

12. A mounted King Swein 'Forkbeard' and his soldiers invade England and oppress its people in 1013, while Queen Emma flees with her young sons, the æthelings Edward and Alfred, to safety in Normandy. From Matthew Paris, *The Life of St Edward the Confessor*, c.1240.

13. The opening folio of Archbishop Wulfstan's 'Sermon of the Wolf' (possibly in Wulfstan's own hand), early eleventh century.

14. Æthelred the Unready, seated on his throne and holding a sword, from *The History of the Church of Abingdon*, *c*.1240.

another thegn who appears prominently in witness lists of the 990s, are mentioned in charters as advising the king to restore to Abingdon its liberty and compensate the abbey for lands that the king had taken from it.[11]

In the midst of the viking raids, this second generation of English Benedictine reform produced a remarkable outpouring of hagiographical, theological and political writings. It is to these monks that we owe the survival of the slim corpus of Old English poetry that has come down to us.[12] In the years following their deaths, Dunstan, Oswald and Æthelwold were quickly memorialized by former students with 'lives' designed to demonstrate their sanctity. Byrhtferth, a monk of Ramsey, honoured Oswald, the founder of his abbey, with a saint's life. An anonymous cleric, who designated himself simply as 'B', dedicated his *Life of Dunstan* to Archbishop Ælfric of Canterbury. A few years later, Adelard, a monk of Christ Church, Canterbury, followed it with a second life written in the form of lections to be read aloud during the Night Office. Wulfstan the Cantor, precentor at the Old Minster, Winchester, wrote a highly informative *Life of St Æthelwold* in conjunction with his canonization in 996. Ælfric of Eynsham, who had been a monk of the Old Minster, Winchester, under Bishop Æthelwold, produced a condensed version of Wulfstan's *vita* after his elevation to the abbacy.

The trio of Byrhtferth, Ælfric and Archbishop Wulfstan were by far the pre-eminent authors of Æthelred's reign. The learned polymath Byrhtferth wrote elaborate computistical works, histories and saints' lives in 'hermeneutic' Latin, a flamboyant style designed to impress the reader with its complicated syntax and arcane words derived from

Greek.[13] Ælfric was particularly prolific during his eighteen years (987–1005) as a monk of the abbey of Cerne Abbas, Dorset. At the request of his lay patrons, Æthelmær and his father Ealdorman Æthelweard, Ælfric composed two series of forty *Catholic Homilies* in the vernacular dealing with events in the Christian calendar and church doctrine. His purpose, as he explained in the preface to the first series, was to arm believers against the wiles of the Antichrist, whose coming he thought imminent, with a clear statement of orthodox beliefs in a language that they could understand.[14] He followed with a third series of forty homilies. As Abbot of Eynsham (1005–*c*.1010), Ælfric wrote lives of saints, still more homilies, and letters of spiritual advice to lay and clerical friends. These later works evidenced a growing concern with the devastation wrought by vikings and frustration with King Æthelred's failure to seek good counsel, perhaps reflecting the views of his patron Æthelmær, who had either voluntarily or involuntarily withdrawn from Æthelred's court in 1006.[15]

As abbot, Ælfric also wrote a series of pastoral letters on doctrine for his friend and correspondent Archbishop Wulfstan. Wulfstan, who drew upon Ælfric's work, was almost as prolific a writer of homilies. Even more than Ælfric, Wulfstan wrote in anticipation of the apocalypse, with the goal of reforming and reordering a sinful English nation in preparation for the end time.[16] He interpreted the vikings as a scourge sent by God, and believed that the stability of the kingdom rested upon the strength of the Christian faith. In his most important political work, *The Institutes of Polity* (composed around 1008 and later revised), Wulfstan lays out his ideal of a well-ordered Christian state ruled by a just king with the good counsel of his bishops. Kings are to fear God, love righteousness and respect and protect the rights and privileges of the Church. Bishops, whom Wulfstan calls God's messengers and teachers, are to proclaim justice and forbid injustice, in both their pastoral and secular capacities.[17] Wulfstan's vision of this Christian world order informs the law codes he drafted for Æthelred and Cnut between 1008 and his death in 1023.[18]

The late 990s is also when the cults of Æthelred's sanctified siblings, Edward the Martyr and Edith, began to develop, a process that Æthelred himself actively promoted. In 993, Æthelred, encouraged by Archbishop Sigeric, founded a nunnery at Cholsey dedicated to his martyred brother. With Æthelred's approval, Edith's body was reburied within the nunnery of Wilton in 997 in recognition of her sanctity. Four years later, Æthelred asked the same of the nuns of Shaftesbury for his brother. The ceremony, presided over by the local bishop Wulfsige of Sherborne, took place against the backdrop of yet another serious viking threat, which probably explains Æthelred's absence. The king, however, demonstrated his gratitude by giving to the nuns land at Bradford-on-Avon, which, if the charter recording this gift is authentic, was to serve as a place of refuge for the nuns and his brother's remains in the event of viking attack on the nunnery.[19] Æthelred's support for his murdered brother's cult may reflect his personal belief in Edward's sanctity, and perhaps even a touch of guilt, but it also carried political benefits. Having siblings venerated as saints enhanced the king's prestige and reinforced the message of his penitential charters: freed from the *unræd* of wicked advisers who had taken advantage of his youthful ignorance, he had matured into a pious king, committed to fulfilling his oath to preserve the peace of the Church and of his realm.

It would be a mistake to dismiss Æthelred's penitential charters and his promotion of the cult of Edward the Martyr as mere propaganda. Æthelred had been taught by his ecclesiastical tutors that the physical conditions of his kingdom and its people reflected God's favour or wrath. Æthelred's reign, as he acknowledged in the charter restoring Abingdon's liberty, had been marked by a series of tribulations. On top of the viking raids there had been an outbreak of murrain in 986 serious enough to warrant comment in the *Anglo-Saxon Chronicle*. The *Chronicle*'s entry for that year is brief: the king harried the bishopric of Rochester; later a pestilence broke out among the cattle. For the Chronicler the two events were clearly connected. Æthelred may have thought so as well after the trauma of Maldon and the military fiasco of the following year. Historians explain the viking raids on England in the 980s with reference to economic and political developments in Britain, Scandinavia and (in some cases) the Caliphate of Baghdad. For Æthelred, the explanation was more personal. A king and his people who failed to act justly and show due reverence to the Church could expect divine punishment.[20] For ecclesiastics and laymen alike, kingship was not merely a secular office and the king not just the lay ruler of a people. An anointed king was Christ's vicar on earth, placed by God over a people to be its shepherd.[21] He was the embodiment of his people, and, as the Old Testament taught, the sins of a king were visited upon the nation.

This was the message of one of the most popular tracts of the time, *De Duodecim Abusivis Saeculi* (Concerning the Twelve Abuses of the World). This short moral and political treatise, written by an anonymous Irish cleric in the seventh century but long attributed to Saint Cyprian, warns of the consequences of having a wicked king. If a ruler fails to fulfil his duties to uphold justice, protect the weak, protect the Church and defend his country, his land will be devastated by enemy armies, diseases that strike down both children and cattle, and tempests that destroy crops and trees.[22] The homilist Ælfric of Eynsham made an abridged translation in which he kept most of the Ninth Abuse, that of the wicked king. Ælfric concisely summarized the Latin text's litany of woes, writing that a wicked ruler 'will very often be made wretched both by attack and by hunger, by pestilence and bad weather and wild animals'.[23] Archbishop Wulfstan copied the treatise's admonitions about kingship into his commonplace book.[24] It would be surprising if Æthelred were unfamiliar with the treatise. As we have seen, he believed that God had sent the vikings as a scourge to lead him and his people back to the path of righteousness. God had to be appeased. A pastoral letter that Ælfric sent to Bishop Wulfsige (d. 1002) alludes to a meeting of the bishops at which they decreed fasts for the 'whole nation' and a mass 'against the pagans' (*contra paganos*) to be sung every Wednesday in every minster and church.[25] Years later, in 1009, when everything he had tried to counter the vikings had failed, Æthelred would seek divine support by imposing a more extensive national programme of penance and alms.[26] That too would fail.

5
Law and (Dis)order

In a macabre sense, the Saint Brice's Day Massacre is a reminder of the precocity of English royal government in the late tenth century. Æthelred was the only king in Western Christendom in 1002 who could reasonably expect that his decrees would be conveyed throughout his kingdom and perhaps even obeyed. Æthelred was the heir to a West Saxon dynasty that over the course of the tenth century had used diplomacy and conquest to fuse Wessex, Mercia, Northumbria and the Danelaw into the 'kingdom of the English'. This was a gradual process, and it would be misleading to see Æthelred's England as a unified state. England during his reign was still a composite kingdom of four 'nations', each with its own sense of identity, customs and laws. The acceptance by all four regions of Æthelred as king was the cement that united the kingdom. What enabled him to be king in more than name was a system of government that his predecessors had created to consolidate their conquests, and royal control of the Church. The reign of Æthelred's father, King Edgar, marked a watershed in the development of both. By the late tenth century, royal government in England had developed to the point that the king and his agents could intrude themselves into the lives of ordinary people probably to a greater degree than anywhere else in Western Christendom.[1] None the less, the power of a king was dependent upon the willing co-operation of the secular and ecclesiastical elites, all of whom, in one manner or another, served as agents of the crown. This dependency was particularly true of the king's rule in Northumbria and the Danelaw, regions that he rarely visited and where his presence was largely restricted to his stylized portrait and name on coins.

Coinage provides the best evidence of the effectiveness of Æthelred's government.[2] Since King Edgar's reign, English coinage had been royal and standardized and Æthelred jealously guarded his monopoly on this. No one but he was permitted to have a moneyer. The activities of moneyers and the quality of the currency were tightly regulated. A moneyer who struck false coins risked the loss of a hand, which was to be nailed above his mint as a warning to others.[3] The penalty for using forged dies or striking coins outside a designated mint town was death or, if the king was merciful, the payment of one's wergild – that is, the monetary value of the malefactor's life as set by law. The same was true for merchants who knowingly used coins deficient in weight or quality and port-reeves who abetted them.[4] Whether such draconian penalties were actually imposed is questionable, but the threat seems to have been effective in light of how few forged coins have been found.[5]

The highly monetarized nature of England's vigorous commercial economy in the late tenth and early eleventh centuries required millions of pennies.[6] These were produced through a network of about ninety mint places, most of which were located in southern England. The importance of protecting the money supply led to removal of mints from vulnerable towns to more secure 'emergency' boroughs built on top of reoccupied Iron Age hill forts. Thus the mint of Chichester was transferred to Cissbury Ring; Wilton to Old Sarum; and Ilchester to South Cadbury. Tribute payments to viking fleets also spurred the production of coins. If the figures given by the Chronicler are trustworthy, the English paid nearly £190,000 to various viking fleets during Æthelred's reign; more if one adds local peacemaking efforts.[7] Much of this tribute was paid in the form of hack silver (fragments of silver items used either as currency or subsequently melted down for reuse) and gold church plate, but if just half was in coins, this would mean that over twenty million silver pennies were given to vikings.[8] That the English people could pay so great a sum is an indication of the country's surplus wealth. (Ironically, the cost to the economy may have been offset to a degree by vikings spending their ill-gotten gains on English goods.) That Æthelred's government could both produce that many coins and extract that much money from its subjects is testimony to its capabilities.

Perhaps most remarkable was the ability of Æthelred's government periodically to recall and remint most, if not all, the silver pennies in circulation. This was made possible by tight royal control over the production and distribution of standardized dies. Numismatists have identified twelve separate coin types issued during Æthelred's reign, some of which were short-lived and circulated perhaps only locally.[9] It is difficult to know what prompted the decision to change

coin types, although in some cases the designs chosen by
the king in consultation with his advisers were clearly
intended to convey timely ideological messages.[10] The 'Helmet' issue, which represented Æthelred as a martial Roman
emperor, is dated to *c.*1003–6 when the viking raids began
to intensify. The short-lived *Agnus Dei* type was issued in
conjunction with the programme of national penance
ordered by the king at Bath in 1009 after the failure of an
ambitious naval build-up the previous year.[11] More generally, the iconography of Æthelred's coinage conveyed the
message that he was a true Christian king. On the obverse
of the coin would be a stylized portrait of him modelled on
Roman coins, which would be encircled by the inscription,
Æthelred rex Anglorum. The reverse would bear Christian
symbols, such as the Hand of God and/or a cross, along
with the names of the moneyer and the mint at which the
coin was struck.

At the centre of government was the king and his council,
the witan, made up of ecclesiastical and secular magnates.
Assemblies were summoned by the king as the need arose,
and were held at or near royal estates and urban palaces,
almost all of which were in southern England. There
Æthelred and his counsellors discussed all manner of royal
and ecclesiastical business, including the appointment or
removal of ealdormen, the 'election' of bishops and abbots,
revisions to the coinage, the promulgation of laws, adjudi-
cation of charges brought against those too powerful to be
dealt with by local officials and the granting of estates by
the king to laymen and churches.[12] Meetings of the council
were also ceremonial events. Held on feast days of the

Christian calendar, royal assemblies enabled Æthelred to display his majesty and personally interact with local landowners, reinforcing their pledges of loyalty and love to him.[13]

The king ruled through a network of royal officials consisting of ealdormen and bishops (who were possessed of secular as well as spiritual authority), royal reeves and king's thegns. In the early tenth century, port- or town-reeves represented royal interests in towns and rural reeves managed the king's estates. The expansion of the ealdormen's sphere of jurisdiction led to the introduction of the offices of high-reeve and shire-reeve (or sheriff), who, like ealdormen, had military as well as administrative and legal duties. King's thegns were wealthy landowners who were personally commended to the king and under his protection (*mund*). Their high social status was reflected in a wergild and oath valued at six times that of a commoner (*ceorl*). Tenth-century rulers regarded them as royal agents. They served as suitors in the courts of shire and hundred, and as 'land-lords' (*landrican*) were responsible for ensuring the lawful behaviour of their tenants and the performance of public services owed from their land holdings, the most important of which were the three military 'common burdens' of '*fyrd*-service', repair of fortifications and maintenance of bridges.[14] Royal and church dues, as well as military service, were rated on the basis of fiscal units known as 'hides' in Wessex and English Mercia, and 'carucates' throughout most of the Danelaw. A hide was a notional 120 acres of land, but the number of real acres comprised by the hide could vary greatly according to the quality of the arable land or the degree of favour in which the king held the landowner.

Most if not all the kingdom during the reign of Æthelred was divided into shires, which were further subdivided into administrative units known as hundreds in Wessex, Mercia and East Anglia, and wapentakes in the northern Danelaw. The shiring of Mercia and the east Midlands probably began in the early decades of the tenth century with the military conquests of King Edward the Elder, the Lady Æthelflæd and King Æthelstan, but may not have been completed until well into Æthelred's reign. As the original function of shires was military, the shires of Mercia were organized around fortified towns, from which they took their names. Presided over by royal officials, the courts of the shire, hundred and borough (that is, a town with fortifications) followed legal procedures prescribed by royal law codes. By the reign of Edgar, hundred courts met every four weeks to witness commercial exchanges, especially the sale of livestock, and to adjudicate disputes.[15] Borough courts were required to meet three times a year, and shire courts twice a year.[16] In each, juries of reputable local men gave testimony in disputes brought by their neighbours. In the hundreds and wapentakes of the Danelaw, twelve thegns were chosen to bring accusations against suspected criminals.

Although the law recognized the value of written evidence, and property disputes often turned on the ability of one of the parties to produce a royal charter proving title, the outcome of most suits depended upon the reputation, social standing and social connections of the accuser and accused. This was especially true when a man was required to produce 'oath helpers' to substantiate his claims. Even cases decided by ordeal were as much appeals to local sentiment as to divine judgement. The ordeal of hot iron and water is a case in point. After taking communion and swearing on relics to his innocence, the accused plunged his hand up to his wrist into boiling water blessed by a priest and lifted from the cauldron an iron bar weighing one pound, which he would then carry nine feet, twelve of his supporters standing on one side and twelve of his accusers on the other. Three days later the hand would be unwrapped to ascertain whether 'it has become discoloured or remained clean'. Men took seriously oaths on holy relics, and the witnesses to an ordeal were blessed with holy water and supposed to have fasted and abstained from sex the night before to impress upon them that the judgement was God's. But ultimately it was up to the attending clergy and onlookers to determine whether the accused had passed or failed the ordeal.[17]

Law and order rested on the dual foundation of community and lordship. In the absence of a police force, the prevention and punishment of crime was an obligation borne by both a man's neighbours and his lord. Homicide was seen as the concern of kinsmen, and the obligation to avenge a death was uncontested, although tenth-century kings and churchmen did their best to limit violence by setting rules for feuds, establishing sanctuaries and brokering settlements. Dealing with theft was a communal responsibility.[18] At the age of twelve, a free male was required to take an oath in the presence of the men of his hundred that he would neither conceal acts of theft nor aid thieves. Lords were expected to exercise discipline over their commended men and those whose land fell within their jurisdiction; in return they received either a share or all of the fines incurred by their men. But oaths could be ignored, and lords could not always be trusted to choose justice over their duty to protect their men, especially those belonging to their households. What truly ensured law and order was the institution of surety.[19] By Cnut's reign and probably before, every free man was required to belong to a 'tithing', a group of ten men who stood surety for the lawful behaviour of each other. If one committed a crime, the other nine were obliged either to bring him to justice or pay compensation for their failure to do so.[20] The pursuit of thieves was a communal responsibility that went beyond the tithing. It was the duty of the chief official of the hundred or a king's village reeve to raise a posse to pursue cattle thieves. If the thief made it to a neighbouring hundred, the chief man of that hundred was obliged to take up the pursuit. This was, at least, what the law prescribed. To encourage individuals to undertake the dangerous and arduous task of pursuing thieves and bringing defiant wrongdoers to justice, tenth-century kings both threatened fines for non-compliance and dangled the prospect of a share of the criminal's confiscated property.[21]

Æthelred was a prolific legislator. He issued at least six law codes over the course of his reign, seven if one counts the Treaty of Andover and its appendix on vouching to warranty.[22] Lawgiving was both a symbolic and practical expression of good kingship. The purpose of royal lawgiving was to 'further Christianity and enhance kingship, profit the people and command respect, bring about peace and settlements, terminate disputes and improve all public behaviour'.[23] The words may have been Wulfstan's, but the authority behind them was Æthelred's. Æthelred's three earliest codes, probably all issued in the 990s, deal with secular matters. *I Æthelred* and *III Æthelred*, issued respectively at Woodstock and Wantage, seem to form a pair, the first addressed to areas under 'English law' and the latter to those under 'Danish law', presumably the 'Five Boroughs' of Leicester, Stamford, Derby, Nottingham and Lincoln. Both are secular codes issued 'to promote peace' and are concerned with ensuring the need for each man to have a surety from his neighbourhood to 'hold him to the performance of every legal duty' and that lords serve as sureties for the men of their households.[24] Although *II Æthelred* is the text of a treaty, it also includes clauses dealing with the theft of cattle and has an appendix concerned with establishing ownership by vouching to warranty.[25] *IV Æthelred* is a composite text that addresses the legal concerns of the burgesses of London. The 'code' (which lacks an introduction) begins with commercial regulations, follows that with laws dealing with tolls and breaches of the peace, and concludes with legislation on coinage.[26] By legislating, Æthelred was fulfilling the oaths he had taken as a child at his coronation to protect the Christian faith, to promote justice by forbidding 'robbery and all unrighteous things to all orders' and 'to command justice and mercy in all judgements'.[27]

Fulfilment of his pledge to provide true peace to the Church and the people of his realm may have been beyond the ability of any tenth-century king, let alone one whose realm was ravaged year in and year out by vikings. Æthelred did not possess the coercive mechanisms needed to ensure an orderly society. The effectiveness of the late Anglo-Saxon state depended on the partnership between the king and the landowning aristocracy. Tenth-century English kings had difficulty imposing their will on recalcitrant subjects, especially if they were members of powerful families. Æthelred could do little to prevent abuses committed by royal agents entrusted with administering justice beyond pious admonitions and threats.[28] Æthelred, as one law code admits, 'frequently and often commanded' a stop to 'unjust practices' such as falsely 'attaching' livestock, refusing to allow trustworthy witnesses to testify, and allowing claims against heirs that were never raised against the previous owner.[29] Archbishop Wulfstan in his *Institutes of Polity* bemoaned that since King Edgar's death there had been more thieves than righteous people serving as royal reeves.[30]

There is no better evidence for both the aspirations and limitations of Æthelred's governance than an Old English memorandum attached to a Latin charter, Sawyer 877, dated 993.[31] The story it tells – of a king's thegn named Wulfbald who repeatedly defied the judgements of royal courts, including a meeting of the witan – serves as a much-needed corrective to the sometimes exaggerated claims made for the judicial power of the late Anglo-Saxon state.[32] A distinctive feature of the charters issued by King Æthelred is that they often include explanations of how the king obtained the land that he was granting. In a number of instances, the narratives refer to crimes committed by the former owners that led to forfeiture of the land.[33] Sawyer 877 records a grant by King Æthelred II to his mother Ælfthryth of an estate at Brabourne and five other properties in Kent that had been forfeited to the crown by Wulfbald because of the misdeeds that he had committed during the first decade of Æthelred's reign. Wulfbald, we are told, ignored two royal commands to return property that he had looted from his stepmother, and two others to restore an estate that he had seized from a kinsman. According to a law, the penalty for disregarding the judgement of a court four times was the forfeiture of all possessions and outlawry, and a witan that met at London formally assigned all of Wulfbald's property to the king and placed him 'in the king's mercy'.[34]

Despite all of this, Wulfbald died in possession of these lands without ever having made amends. Wulfbald's death set off a bloody battle over the estate of Brabourne, pitting his widow and their son against Wulfbald's uncle's son that resulted in the deaths of a king's thegn and his fifteen companions. That was sufficiently serious to demand that action be taken, and it was then that Wulfbald's possessions finally passed into the hands of the king. On the face of it, the failure to enforce repeated judgements against Wulfbald reflects poorly on Æthelred's legal regime. But, despite historians' recent emphasis upon the effectiveness of the late Anglo-Saxon state, the case of Wulfbald was probably not uncommon. Bringing powerful men to justice was a persistent problem for kings throughout the tenth century, as is evidenced by repeated legislation on this subject.[35] Enforcement of legal judgements was left to the community, and Wulfbald's neighbours probably hesitated to involve themselves in what was an intra-familial dispute. Enforcement was a royal concern in those cases that directly involved the interests of the crown.[36]

Nor did Æthelred always act in accordance with his own laws, as evidenced by his approval of the violation of church sanctuary by the burgesses of Oxford in their eagerness to rid their town of Danes. Less dramatic but more typical is the decision Æthelred rendered in a dispute that arose in 995 between Ealdorman Leofsige of Essex and the port-reeves of Oxford and Buckingham.[37] The ealdorman accused the reeves of Buckingham and Oxford of having defied the law by allowing Christian burial for two brothers who had died defending a thief. Æthelred dismissed the complaint of the ealdorman, explaining that he 'did not wish to distress his dear and precious reeve of Oxford, Æthelwig'. The lands of the two deceased brothers and their surviving sibling, however, were forfeited to the crown.[38] This was an act of royal mercy; it was also testimony to the importance of enjoying royal favour.

As the social and political bonds upon which law and order depended frayed under the strain of viking attacks, the ecclesiastical and lay elite of the realm grew increasingly discontented with Æthelred's governance. By the end of his reign, they had come to question not only Æthelred's competence but his ability to provide justice.

6
Losing the Kingdom

In 1014 Archbishop Wulfstan chastised his fellow country-men in his 'Sermon of the Wolf'. Led astray by the Devil in a world nearing its end, the English people had fallen so deeply into sin as to arouse the anger of God:

> For long now, nothing has prospered here or elsewhere, but in every district there has been harrying and hunger, burning and bloodshed over and again. And stealing and slaughter, plague and pestilence, murrain and disease, slan-der and hatred, and the plundering of robbers have damaged us very severely; and excessive taxes have greatly oppressed us ... for many years now, so it seems, there have been in this country many injustices and unsteady loyalties among men everywhere.

Of the vikings, Wulfstan thundered: 'We pay them con-tinually, and they humiliate us daily ... and indeed, what else is there in all of these events but the wrath of God towards this people?'[1]

Many in Wulfstan's audience would have nodded their heads in assent as the archbishop recited this litany of mis-fortunes. Certainly this would not have been the experience of everyone. But, as exaggerated as it is, Wulfstan's assessment of conditions in England was rooted in a dismal reality. Between 1006 and Æthelred's death in the spring of 1016, England would experience not only devastating viking raids but Danish conquest. Æthelred's court would be the setting for political intrigues, murders and betrayals that provoked a quasi-rebellion by the king's son Edmund. Æthelred would share with King James II the humiliation of exile. His flight to Normandy in 1013 was the consequence of a foreign invasion, and, unlike his Stuart descendant, his exile would be brief, but it is telling that the ecclesiastical and lay magnates of the realm hesitated before inviting him to resume his kingship. When they did, they set as a condition for his return that 'he would govern them more justly than he did before'.[2]

The composition of Æthelred's royal council and household was transformed between 1002 and 1006.[3] In part this was due to natural attrition, as these years witnessed the deaths and replacements of seven bishops, including both archbishops. Two of the thegns who had stood closest to the king in the 990s, Brihtnoth and Wulfric Spot, the brother of Ealdorman Ælfhelm of Northumbria, had also apparently died of natural causes. But other changes observed in the witness lists smack of deliberate policy, not unlike the court purge of 993.[4] In the years 1005 and 1006, the other five leading thegns of the 990s either withdrew or were removed from the royal council. Æthelred's kinsman Æthelmær, the son of the deceased Ealdorman Æthelweard, and the king's uncle Ordulf both chose in 1005 to retire to religious houses that they had founded at Eynsham and Tavistock. Wulfgeat, Wulfheah and Ufegeat were not given a choice. In 1006

Wulfgeat, a 'beloved thegn' who had once admonished Æthelred to restore to Abingdon lands unjustly taken from the abbey, was deprived of his rank and property because, according to John of Worcester, of the 'unjust judgements and arrogant deeds he had perpetrated'.[5] In that same year, Æthelred, holding court at his royal estate at Cookham in Berkshire, ordered the blinding of the brothers Wulfheah and Ufegeat. Their father, Ælfhelm, the ealdorman for southern Northumbria, had recently been murdered. The Chronicler reports simply that he had been 'struck dead' (*of-slagen*). John of Worcester, based either upon local tradition or a lost source, names the culprit, Eadric Streona. Pretending to be the ealdorman's dear friend, Eadric had invited Ælfhelm to go hunting with him in the woods near Shrewsbury. The quarry turned out to be the ealdorman, who was ambushed and killed by Eadric's henchman, the town's executioner.[6]

Although John of Worcester was writing in the 1120s, his account is credible, at least in its basic outline. He knew details absent from the *Chronicle*'s laconic account, most crucially that Wulfheah and Ufegeat were Ealdorman Ælfhelm's sons. John was also well informed about Eadric's familial connections.[7] It stretches credibility to see Ælfhelm's murder and the blinding of his sons by order of the king as unrelated. Unlike their father's death, Wulfheah and Ufegeat's punishment conformed to the law. We are not told the charges against them, but they must have been serious, possibly treason, as bodily mutilation was the merciful alternative to the death penalty.[8] Their blinding would have signalled to the court King Æthelred's acceptance, and perhaps even approval, of their father's killing. This would not be the last time that Æthelred would legitimize a political murder.

Eadric had a motive: Ealdorman Ælfhelm and his sons were obstacles to his political ambitions.[9] Eadric Streona's rise was meteoric. He belonged to a Mercian family of thegnly rank that began to frequent Æthelred's court in the mid 990s. Based on their positions in witness lists, neither his father nor his brothers were particularly close to the king. (They always attested after Wulfheah.[10]) Eadric makes his first appearance in a charter of 1002, in which his is the final name on the witness list.[11] Just five years later, he would be Ealdorman of Mercia, the first to hold that powerful office since Ælfric *cild*'s exile in 985. Ealdorman Ælfhelm, the brother of Wulfric Spot, also belonged to a Mercian family, but one wealthier and more powerful than Eadric's.[12] Without an ealdorman in Mercia, Ælfhelm's sphere of jurisdiction may have extended beyond southern Northumbria to the west Midlands. Because of their wealth and connections, Wulfheah and Ufegeat were Eadric's natural rivals within Mercia. If Eadric was to rise, the family of Ælfhelm had to fall. The power of Ælfhelm's kindred had only been reduced. The nephews of Wulfric Spot, Morcar and Sigeferth, who would later also fall victim to Eadric, emerged as the leading thegns of the Five Boroughs. Ealdorman Ælfhelm's daughter Ælfgifu of Northampton became the first wife and subsequent mistress of King Cnut following his second marriage to Emma of Normandy. It is tempting to think that she may have had something to do with her husband's decision to execute the faithless Eadric.

Æthelred's posthumous byname is not completely unfair. Although he filled episcopal and abbatial vacancies with pious clerics devoted to monasticism and selected Wulfstan to draft his later legislation, he was a poorer judge of character when it came to choosing lay advisers. He admitted as much in 993 when he repudiated the favourites whom he claimed had taken advantage of his 'youthful ignorance' to despoil church lands. Not all his appointments were ill-chosen. Uhtred, son of Earl Waltheof of Bamburgh, became Ealdorman of all Northumbria in 1006 as a reward for the courage and initiative he displayed in relieving a Scottish siege of Durham. Ulfcytel, who bore the duties if not the title of ealdorman in East Anglia, proved to be an inspirational, if not always successful, military leader. But the balance sheet is decidedly not in Æthelred's favour. He exiled two ealdormen for crimes and may have sanctioned the murder of a third. The Chronicler reserves special blame for Ælfric, who held the ealdormanry of Hampshire for nearly Æthelred's entire reign, and the notorious Eadric Streona.

Although Ælfric may not have been as cowardly as the Chronicler made him out to be, Eadric's reputation for guile and treachery seems well deserved. It is difficult to explain his shifting loyalties and betrayals by anything other than self-interest. And Eadric was a creature purely of Æthelred's making. He was not a scion of one of the great families that had dominated higher royal offices during the reigns of Edgar and Edward. Indeed, Eadric's lack of pedigree might have been one of his attractions. Æthelred seems to have been leery of the more powerful aristocratic families. As we have seen, instead of choosing a son or close kinsman to succeed Ealdorman Æthelwine and Ealdorman Æthel-weard, he had left their ealdormanries unfilled. When the king decided to fill the long-vacant office of Ealdorman of Mercia, he chose an obscure king's thegn rather than a member of one of the great Mercian families. Perhaps to compensate for Eadric's modest social status or simply out of affection, Æthelred honoured his new ealdorman with his daughter Eadgyth's hand in marriage. Flouting conven-tion, Æthelred elevated his son-in-law above more senior ealdormen. From 1012 on, Eadric Streona was the leading ealdorman in Æthelred's court.[13] If Eadric turned out to be *unræd* incarnate, Æthelred had no one to blame but himself.

The Saint Brice's Day Massacre was the act of a king con-fident that he could handle the existing viking threat without mercenaries, especially since some of them had proved unre-liable. If that is what King Æthelred believed, he was wrong. In late summer 1006, the level of viking activity intensified once more with the appearance off Sandwich of a 'great fleet' that immediately began to pillage south-eastern England. Æthelred responded by calling up 'the whole nation from Wessex and Mercia'. The English army campaigned without success against the viking host throughout the autumn. Their need for provisions simply made matters worse for local landowners and peasants. After establishing a secure base in the Isle of Wight and establishing supply depots in advance, the viking army in November struck deep into Hampshire and Berkshire, while Æthelred, to the scorn of the Chronicler, was taking food rents in distant Shropshire, which, probably not coincidentally, was where Eadric's lands lay.[14] The English army, however, was still in the field. After cautiously tracking the viking raiders, they finally intercepted them on the banks of the Kennett river as they made their way back to their ships laden with booty. The outcome was yet another English defeat. Once again, King Æthelred and his counsellors reluctantly decided that they had no alternative but to offer their despoilers tribute and provisions. The cost of peace this time came to £36,000.

More money was to be spent on upgrading English defences. Æthelred in 1008 met with the witan to consider what needed to be done before the arrival of the next viking fleet. He was persuaded to undertake an ambitious military build-up and to pacify God by attending more diligently to his sworn duties as king. The basic military strategy adopted in 1008 was preclusive, centring on the construction of a massive royal fleet to intercept raiders at sea. Extending, or possibly reviving, the naval policies of Edgar, Æthelred ordered the kingdom to be divided into 'ship-sokes' (administrative districts) of 300 (or 310) hides to facilitate the construction and maintaining of a great armada.[15] Completely novel was the requirement that a helmet and mail coat be supplied from every eight hides 'unremittingly over all England', which suggests that English levies had hitherto been at a disadvantage against better-armoured vikings.[16] The Chronicler claims that the fleet mustered at Sandwich in the following year was the largest naval force ever assembled by an English king.[17] This may not be hyperbole. Domesday Book records a total of 70,000 hides and carucates, which does not include shires north of Yorkshire, where even in 1086 royal power was limited. If the hidage of England in 1008 was similar, the districts owed the crown over two hundred ships and armour for eight to nine thousand soldier-sailors.

This was Æthelred's most dramatic attempt to shore up the defences of his kingdom, but it was not his only effort. The edict of 1008 complemented an ongoing programme of military construction that may have begun in the 990s. Iron Age hill forts at South Cadbury in Somerset, Old Sarum in Wiltshire, Cissbury in Sussex and Daw's Castle in Somerset were reoccupied and made defensible, and the defences of existing boroughs were refurbished and upgraded.[18] The fosse surrounding Wallingford was enlarged, and the town's northern bank raised and crowned with a stone wall. There is evidence for similar upgrading of defences at Cricklade, Amesbury, Malmesbury, Wareham and Lydford.[19] Æthelred and his advisers understood the importance of coastal defence as well. Maintaining guard ships and keeping watch for unfriendly vessels were added to the duties of thegns who had lands along the coast.[20] The lookout and beacon of St Mary-in-Castro at Dover was constructed to warn against the approach of viking fleets, as was possibly a fortified hilltop lookout at Carisbrooke Castle on the strategic Isle of Wight.[21] Gainsaying the Victorian caricature of Æthelred as a lazy and ill-prepared king, in actuality he and his advisers recognized the deficiencies in his military forces and the kingdom's civil defences and used the powerful institutions of governance of late Saxon England to remedy both.

Between 1009 and 1012, England's defences would be severely challenged by an immense raiding army. King Æthelred's armada failed before even engaging the enemy. In spring or early summer of 1009, King Æthelred posted his new fleet at Sandwich to guard against the return of the vikings. But the naval preparations fell victim to internal dissension when Eadric Streona's brother Brihtric brought an accusation against Wulfnoth *cild*, 'the South Saxon'. The byname suggests that Wulfnoth was a prominent Sussex landowner, and possibly the father of Cnut's powerful Earl of Wessex, Godwine.[22] The accusation may have been political. Factions headed by the ætheling Æthelstan and Eadric were developing within the court, and Wulfnoth's son Godwine was one of the ætheling's favourites.[23] Wulfnoth responded by turning viking: he 'enticed' the crews of twenty ships while he himself began to raid along the southern coast of England. Brihtric's pursuit of the renegades ended in disaster when a storm battered his eighty ships. Those driven ashore by the wind were promptly burnt by Wulfnoth. This fiasco persuaded King Æthelred and his counsellors that it was best to leave the fleet; the surviving ships were brought back to London. As the Chronicler laments, 'we had neither the luck nor the honour that the ship-army was useful to this country, any more than it often was before'.[24]

The disheartening dispersal of the national fleet was followed by the arrival on 1 August of 'an immense raiding army' under the command of Thorkell the Tall, another viking adventurer who, at least according to thirteenth-century saga writers, was the leader of the Jómsvikings, a semi-legendary 'brotherhood' of viking mercenaries whose stronghold supposedly lay on the southern coast of the Baltic Sea. With no fleet to oppose them, they ravaged eastern Kent until they were persuaded to move west by a surprisingly modest £3,000.[25] For the next two months, they pillaged the Isle of Wight, Hampshire and Berkshire. Æthelred responded by assembling the shire forces into a large army, which he distributed along the coastal areas to guard against viking attack. Thorkell's raiders evaded them as they continued to raid, although at one point the full English army led by the king outmanoeuvred the raiders and stood between the vikings and their ships. A battle seemed imminent, though Æthelred chose not to engage. The Chronicler blames this on Eadric, but gives no further explanation. Presumably, Eadric argued that the king did not have a large enough force to guarantee victory. From their base in Kent, the raiders continued to ravage on both sides of the Thames throughout the autumn and winter.

What all could agree upon was that the vikings were a manifestation of God's wrath, and that, to be successful against them, the English had to get right with God. Æthelred was taught by Archbishop Wulfstan and his other clerical advisers that the vikings were God's punishment for the sins of the English people. As the proem to the charter confirming the endowment of the abbey of Eynsham explains, the English people had been suffering 'the fires of war and the pillaging of our wealth ... reducing us almost to destruction'. The remedy was to look 'with diligent care to the needs of our souls' and assuage God's anger 'by a continuous display of God's good works'. Endowing a monastery was one such good work. Legislating against wicked practices was another. This had been Edgar's response to a plague that God had unleashed upon the people to punish them for 'sin and disregard of God's commands'.[26] It was also Æthelred's response to the human plague that God had sent. At a meeting of the witan at Enham in 1008, perhaps the same one that ordered the building of a fleet, Æthelred issued the first of the codes that Archbishop Wulfstan drafted on his behalf.[27] The Enham Code begins with an exhortation to 'love and honour one God, and zealously observe one Christian faith' and to 'confirm by word and by pledge, our firm intention of observing one Christian faith under the authority of one king', and it concludes: 'Let us loyally support one royal lord, and all of us together defend our lives and our country, to the best of our ability, and from our inmost heart pray to God Almighty for help.' In between there are decrees against immoral behaviour by clergy and laity, for the protection of the rights and dues owed the Church, for the proper observation of Christian festivals, and, tucked among these, edicts designed to improve public security (clauses 31–40). These deal with a variety of topics, including currency, weights and measures, repair of fortifications and bridges, fulfilling military service that was owed, preparation of the fleet so that the ships would be ready soon after Easter, desertions from the army, plots against the king, injuries to nuns and widows, and, generally, the suppression of injustice 'in matters both religious and secular'. In short, Æthelred was demonstrating his commitment to fulfilling his coronation oath.

The advent of the 'great raiding army' the following year meant that stiffer spiritual correction was needed. Following Carolingian practice, Æthelred responded with an impressive programme for national repentance, prayer and alms-giving.[28] Echoing the previous year's legislation, the code that Wulfstan drafted for Æthelred at Bath in 1009 began with the admonition that 'one God shall be loved and honoured above all, and all men shall show obedience to their king in accordance with best traditions of their ancestors and cooperate with him in defending the realm'.[29] The legislation enjoined every adult Christian to give alms, fast and pray, and prescribed the litanies the clergy were to chant to obtain the divine favour necessary for victory. In the wake of the Battle of Maldon, Æthelred had embraced the role of the penitent king, the Church's prodigal son. By 1009 the fires of Maldon had spread into a conflagration that threatened to consume the entire kingdom. Æthelred and his bishops now called upon all the English people to make amends and seek God's forgiveness for their many sins. A litany preserved in the early eleventh-century Winchester Troper explains that the prayers were needed so that God 'may see fit to preserve King Æthelred and the army of the English'. These litanies 'against the pagans' (*contra paganos*) generally concluded with the three-fold invocation of the Lamb of God calling upon Christ to 'grant us peace'. Simon Keynes and Rory Naismith make a convincing case for associating the limited *Agnus Dei* coin issue with Æthelred's national programme and the enforced litanies.[30]

Æthelred's programme of repentance, prayer and alms-giving was no more effective than the ship-sokes had been. Even with helmets and coats of mail, English *fyrd*men proved no match for Thorkell's war-tested vikings. After defeating Ulfcytel of East Anglia and the men of Cambridgeshire in battle at Ringmere in May 1010, Thorkell's vikings spent the next six months ravaging East Anglia, the east Midlands and Wessex without significant resistance, before returning to their base in Kent. According to the Chronicler, King Æthelred summoned his witan for advice about how the country should be defended, but he vacillated – whatever policy the king adopted would be discarded within a few weeks for another. The Chronicler attributes the inability of the English to deal with Thorkell to the king's and his counsellors' poor timing and inconstancy of purpose.[31] The humiliation of the English culminated in 1011 with Thorkell's forces capturing and sacking Canterbury, attributed by the Chronicler to the treachery of a cleric, and the taking prisoner of Archbishop Ælfheah.[32] The king and the witan, meeting in London at Easter in 1012, agreed to pay a massive tribute of £48,000. Archbishop Ælfheah's refusal to allow any ransom to be paid for him won him martyrdom. Angry and drunken vikings reportedly pelted Ælfheah with the gnawed bones of cattle until one of them struck the archbishop on the head with the butt of his axe, killing him. This had apparently not been Thorkell's intention, for he allowed the bishops of London and Dorchester to take the archbishop's body back to London, where he was buried with all due honours in the church of St Paul.[33]

Once paid, Thorkell's fleet dispersed and the various *lith*s returned to their respective homes – all except for forty-five ships. Incapable of mounting any effective military resistance to Thorkell, Æthelred decided to try the mercenary route once more, and somehow managed to persuade the viking captain that it would be more profitable to eat from a king's table than to steal food from it.

Thorkell agreed that he and the forty-five ships under his personal command would defend Æthelred's realm in return for being fed and clothed. To fulfil his end of the bargain, Æthelred instituted a regular tax, the much-hated impost known as the *heregeld* (army tax).[34]

Swein's return to England the following year may have been prompted by Thorkell's alliance with the English king. Thorkell is a shadowy figure. His early career is obscured by the legends that grew up about him in the following centuries. What seems certain is that he acted as an independent agent, much like the viking sea kings of the ninth century. Like Olaf Tryggvason, Thorkell represented a potential threat to the Danish king's Scandinavian hegemony.

Swein's expedition of 1013 was fundamentally different from his previous assaults on England. This time he came to conquer rather than merely raid. Using his position as King of Denmark and the wealth he had previously acquired in England, he recruited a large naval force. The captains and complements of most of the *lith*s probably were Danes, but, as in his previous expeditions, he attracted followers from throughout Scandinavia, drawn by the prospect of pay and loot. This was not a 'national army', despite being led by a king. It was, however, an army of conquest.

Possibly because Thorkell's fleet guarded the mouth of the Thames, Swein began his campaign in the north. He had quick success in compelling the submissions of Northumbria, Lindsey and the Five Boroughs and other regions of the Danelaw, which he secured through the taking of hostages. The fragile unity of the kingdom of England was fracturing, as regional magnates sought to come to terms with the invaders. The submissions of Oxford and Winchester followed, as Swein marched south towards London, the key to the kingdom. But the Londoners, buoyed by the presence of King Æthelred and Thorkell, and confident in the city's defences, defied Swein. Rather than wasting time and troops in a long, drawn-out siege, Swein turned westwards to reduce to submission those regions that were still loyal to Æthelred. After Ealdorman Æthelmær submitted to him at Bath, a city rich in imperial symbolism, Swein returned to his ships in the north. He did not need to threaten London with attack. Now isolated, the city leaders sent messengers north offering their submission. Abandoned by his ealdormen and the burgesses of London, Æthelred retreated to Thorkell's fleet on the Thames. His intention was to continue the fight, but first he despatched Bishop Ælfhun of London to escort his wife Emma and their children, the æthelings Edward and Alfred, to the queen's brother in Normandy. His diplomatic marriage had been contracted to close Normandy's ports to viking raiders. It now filled a far different need, providing Æthelred with a place of refuge for a court in exile.

By this time, Swein, although not consecrated, had been accepted as king by most of the English magnates. In a reversal of roles, Æthelred made his base with the mercenary fleet in the Isle of Wight. While Swein collected provisions and continued to raid in the north, Thorkell did the same in the south. The English people were caught in the middle between two harrying armies. In the spring, Æthelred acknowledged the reality of the situation and sailed off to Normandy. The sources are silent about whether Æthelred's two eldest sons by his first wife, the æthelings Æthelstan and Edmund, remained in England or joined their father in exile. One cannot even be certain whether Æthelstan was even still alive.[35]

Æthelred's flight resolved any lingering doubts. Swein was now King of England as well as Denmark and the line of English kings was broken, but his reign was brief. He died a few months later, on 3 February 1014. The Danish fleet and the chief men of Lindsey at Gainsborough, in Lincolnshire, immediately acclaimed his son Cnut as king. At the same time, the lay and ecclesiastical magnates of England had gathered at York for what would have been Swein's first meeting of the witan. The main purpose was consecrating a new Bishop of London, but news of Swein's death changed the agenda.[36] The question that faced the magnates now was: Æthelred or Cnut? For Archbishop Wulfstan and the bishops, this was a foregone conclusion. It was the duty of bishops to guide kings and to chastise them if they failed to fulfil their duties as a Christian ruler. But an anointed ruler was God's chosen, and as such was sacrosanct. In the 'Sermon of the Wolf', a version of which Wulfstan may have preached at the assembly, the archbishop condemned his countrymen for having perpetrated two great betrayals of earthly lordship. They had plotted against and killed King Edward, and they had driven Æthelred from his land.[37] Even an unjust ruler could not be rightly deposed.

The ealdormen and king's thegns may have been more conflicted. Not only had they submitted to Swein and pledged him loyalty, but Cnut still held the hostages they had given his father as a guarantee of good faith. But their submissions to Swein had been coerced, and, as the bishops would have reminded them, they had all sworn oaths first to support and honour their royal lord King Æthelred. It is not surprising that the witan chose Æthelred over Cnut. That they did so with reservations is more surprising. They sent a message to Æthelred assuring him that no lord was dearer to them than their natural lord, and they would joyfully receive him back, if he would promise to 'govern them more justly than he had in the past'.

Even more telling was Æthelred's response. He sent envoys, including his eldest son by Emma, Edward, a boy of ten or eleven years, to convey his acceptance:

> He ordered [them] to greet all his people, and said that he would be a gracious lord to them, and would improve each of the things which they all hated; and all the things that had been said and done against him should be forgiven, on condition that they all unanimously turned to him without treachery.[38]

The opening words 'Het gretan ealne leodscipe' recall the language of royal writs, and it is possible that the Chronicler drew upon Æthelred's formal announcement to the nation. One can only speculate about 'the things which ... all [his subjects] hated', though the sources may provide some hints.

In the great secular law code that Wulfstan would draft for Cnut, the new Danish king promised that his reeves would provide for him in accordance with the law, taking only the food rents owed by royal manors. No longer would they compel landowners to give the king what they did not lawfully owe him.[39] Wulfstan in his writings showed particular concern about corrupt reeves. Anglo-Saxon kings could and did

legislate against reeves who abused their authority, but polic-
ing and disciplining those who acted in the king's name was
difficult in the best of times and nearly impossible in the cha-
otic conditions created by recurring viking raids. Excessive
royal exactions undoubtedly were also high on the list, as
were complaints about ill-conceived or poorly implemented
policies.[40] One suspects that many landowners thought
Æthelred overly eager to find reasons to confiscate property.
Others may have been uneasy about the violence that had
plagued the king's court. Quite simply, the elites of the realm
wanted the king to conduct himself more lawfully.

The restoration of the monarchy during the Lenten sea-
son (16 March to 24 April) of 1014 was finally secured by
reciprocal oaths. The first edict issued by Æthelred and his
witan was to declare every Danish king henceforth an out-
law in England. Emboldened by the sworn support of the
nobility and needing to demonstrate his worthiness to be
king, Æthelred seized the initiative and marched north
at the head of a large army to confront Cnut in Lindsey. At
his approach, Cnut set sail for Denmark, putting ashore
at Sandwich long enough to deposit his hostages, whose
hands, ears and noses he ordered to be chopped off. The
act was calculated both to exhibit Cnut's Christian mercy
by his sparing of the hostages and to inspire terror. The
mutilated hostages were living testimonials to Cnut's resolution. Æthelred contented himself with ravaging Lindsey
as brutally as any viking. Unlike his earlier dealings with
mercenaries, Æthelred had benefited from his agreement
with Thorkell. He and his men had proved loyal throughout the crisis of the previous year. This loyalty, however,

did not come cheap. In 1014 Æthelred had to raise £21,000 through taxes to pay the wages he owed them.

Æthelred had sworn to forgo vengeance against those who had turned against him. He appears to have disregarded this pledge in his dealings with the brothers Sigeferth and Morcar, the foremost king's thegns in the Five Boroughs. The brothers were the nephews of Wulfric Spot and kinsmen of Ealdorman Ælfhelm. Anger and resentment against the ill-treatment of their kinsmen may have made them more ready to throw in with Swein. They had not only submitted to him, along with the other leading men of the Danelaw, but had established personal bonds with the Danish king by approving the marriage of their sister Ælfgifu to Cnut. Given these ties, Æthelred may have distrusted the brothers' renewed pledges of loyalty. Eadric's relations with Sigeferth and Morcar were even more uneasy. They were kinsmen of a man he had killed. He was protected from their vengeance by the favour of the king, but they were at the very least a potential threat.[41] He dealt with them as he had with Ælfhelm. According to the Chronicler, Eadric lured the brothers into his chambers, where he murdered them. This apparently was a judicial murder performed with Æthelred's approval. The king gave his imprimatur by ordering the property of the murdered thegns to be confiscated and Sigeferth's widow seized and brought into the nunnery of Malmesbury.[42]

Edmund, the king's eldest surviving son, had different ideas. Acting quickly, he married the widow before she could be forced to take the veil, and secured possession of Sigeferth's property. According to the Chronicler, the leading men of the Five Boroughs submitted to him, as they had done before to Swein. Edmund had established an independent power base in the Danelaw in opposition to his father. This looks very much as though Edmund was in revolt, but whether it was against his father or Eadric is unclear. Concerns about the succession may underlie Edmund's actions. His position in 1014 was the same as Edward the Martyr's had been in 975. He was the king's eldest son by a first wife, and had two half-brothers, Edward and Alfred, whose mother was the king's consort and a consecrated queen. In a few years, Edward would be old enough to be a credible candidate for the throne, especially if his father signalled that he was his heir. Edmund may have been shoring up support for his succession. By marrying Sigeferth's widow, Edmund also assumed from his deceased brother Æthelstan leadership of the court faction opposed to Eadric.[43]

In the autumn of 1015, Cnut returned with a fleet of 160 ships to raid the south of England. Edmund responded by raising an army in the north, intending to join forces with Eadric Streona, and confront Cnut with their combined power. Edmund, however, grew suspicious of Eadric's intentions and returned north without engaging Cnut. In mid-winter, Cnut, now with the open support of Eadric Streona, began a systematic campaign of conquest. His strategy was simple: he would ravage a territory until the demoralized local leaders submitted to his authority, and then move on to the next shire. The obvious strategic response was to raise an army, force Cnut into battle and destroy his forces. King Æthelred, never comfortable with military command and in failing health, was unwilling or incapable of taking the field. Edmund attempted to fill the vacuum. The first army that he raised in the name of his father dispersed when it became clear that the king had no intention of joining it. A second 'national army' disintegrated when King Æthelred abandoned it because of rumours that he was to be betrayed. While Edmund and Ealdorman Uhtred of Northumbria were teaching the men of Staffordshire, Shropshire and Leicestershire with fire and sword that they had made a grave error in submitting to Cnut, and Cnut and Eadric were ravaging east Midland shires loyal to Edmund, King Æthelred lay in failing health in London. He was, none the less, still king and London was still the centre of the kingdom. Like a magnet, king and city drew the rivals towards them. Edmund arrived in time to attend his dying father. By the time Cnut's fleet entered the Thames, the king was dead, and the witan had acclaimed Edmund as England's new king.

On 23 April 1016, King Æthelred was buried in the church of St Paul the Apostle with honours appropriate to a king. The Chronicler's obituary is short and to the point: 'He ended his days on Saint George's Day, and he had held his kingdom with great toil and difficulties as long as his life lasted.'44

Epilogue and Conclusion

His father's death and his anointing as king freed Edmund to mount a forceful resistance, one which earned him the byname 'Ironside'. As Cnut continued to ravage across Mercia, East Anglia and Northumbria, King Edmund raised a large army. He pursued Cnut and brought him to battle, inconclusively, at Penselwood in Somerset and then at Sherston in Wiltshire. A third battle at 'Assandun' in Essex proved decisive.[1] Edmund lost the battle when Ealdorman Eadric Streona, who had ostensibly returned to Edmund's side, treacherously left the battlefield with his forces.[2] Edmund, who had probably been wounded in this or one of the previous battles, was forced to sign a treaty with Cnut, conceding to the Dane all of England north of Wessex. When Edmund died about a month later, Cnut became king of all England, bringing to an end the viking wars.

Æthelred's reign of nearly thirty-eight years was the longest of any Anglo-Saxon ruler. If he had died in AD 1000, history would have remembered him more kindly. His story might have been that of a child-king's who, after a misspent youth, matured and embraced his father Edgar's commitment to monastic reform. He ruled a prosperous and well-ordered kingdom. The vikings would have played a subordinate role in this narrative, with the defeat at Maldon perhaps a catalyst for Æthelred's spiritual awakening and harbinger of things to come in his successor's reign. But Æthelred lived for sixteen more years, and during that time conditions steadily worsened as England suffered under wave upon wave of destructive viking raids, until one became a campaign of conquest.

However, the military failures and ultimate defeat of the English cannot be blamed on their king's lack of effort or reluctance to act. Æthelred's actions were those of an energetic ruler committed to the defence of his kingdom and willing to try whatever might work. But the military challenges were great. England had enjoyed peace for a generation and its military defences were ill-prepared to counter this hydra-headed enemy, as early defeats in the field dramatically revealed. Tribute, if paid in a timely fashion, was a prudent response, but it bought only a respite. Even if that fleet dispersed, it or a new one would appear the following year, encouraged by previous successes. The size of the kingdom of the English made it difficult to defend, and its fusion of Wessex, Mercia and the Danelaw was recent and still incomplete. Even given England's precocious governmental development, the ability of the king to exert his will grew weaker the further one receded from the kingdom's West Saxon core. Æthelred had to rely on loyal, competent ealdormen and reeves to rule and to defend the realm, and too many of them proved to be neither. In part this was his fault: he was not the best judge of character, at least when it came to filling secular offices. He was also unable or unwilling to contain familial rivalries among the kingdom's nobility, a problem that had plagued his predecessor's reign, and either turned a blind eye towards or condoned extrajudicial violence committed by favourites. This helps explain why so many looked to their self-interest and submitted to Swein and Cnut, despite the oaths of loyalty they had sworn to Æthelred. Most directly, the failure was military. Æthelred might be criticized for his reluctance to lead troops in the field. But his and his advisers' greatest deficiency was a lack of a coherent strategic vision. One may question the Chronicler's theme of treachery and disloyalty, yet he was a keen observer and appreciated that the root cause of defeat was not the policies but their faulty implementation and the inconstancy with which they were followed. As a result,

> When the enemy was in the east, then the army was in the west; and when they were in the south, then our army was in the north. Then all the counsellors were ordered to the king, and it then had to decide how this country should be defended. But whatever was then decided, it did not stand for even a month. In the end there was no head man who wanted to gather an army, but each fled as best as he could; nor in the end would one shire help another.[3]

Notes

In quotations from Old English and Latin sources, I have used what I consider to be the best published translations of these works but have felt free to emend them where necessary.

ABBREVIATIONS

ASC	*The Anglo-Saxon Chronicle* (cited by year and manuscript letter). The English translations are from Michael Swanton, *The Anglo-Saxon Chronicle* (New York: Routledge, 1996)
ASE	*Anglo-Saxon England* (journal)
Attestations	Simon Keynes, *An Atlas of Attestations in Anglo-Saxon Charters, c.670–1066* (Cambridge: Department of Anglo-Saxon, Norse and Celtic Studies, University of Cambridge, 2002), cited by table
Diplomas	Simon Keynes, *The Diplomas of King Æthelred the Unready, 978–1016* (Cambridge: Cambridge University Press, 1980)
Edgar, King of the English	Donald Scragg (ed.), *Edgar, King of the English, 959–975* (Woodbridge: Boydell & Brewer, 2008)
EHD	*English Historical Documents: Volume I: c.500–1042*, ed. Dorothy Whitelock, 2nd edn (London: Routledge, 1979).
EHR	*English Historical Review* (journal)
JW	*The Chronicle of John of Worcester*, vol. 2, ed. R. R. Darlington and P. McGurk (Oxford: Oxford University Press, 1995)
Keynes, 'An Abbot'	Simon Keynes, 'An Abbot, an Archbishop and the Viking Raids of 1006–7 and 1009–12', *ASE*, 36 (2007), pp. 151–220
Lavelle	Ryan Lavelle, *Æthelred II: King of the English 978–1016* (Stroud: Tempus, 2002)
Laws	*The Laws of the Kings of England from Edmund to Henry I*, ed. and trans. A. J. Robertson (Cambridge: Cambridge University Press, 1925)
Life of St Oswald	Byrhtferth, *Life of St Oswald*, in *Byrhtferth of Ramsey: The Lives of St Oswald and St Ecgwine*, ed. and trans. Michael Lapidge (Oxford: Oxford University Press, 2009)
Making of English Law	Patrick Wormald, *The Making of English Law: King Alfred to the Twelfth Century* (Oxford: Blackwell, 1999)
Maldon, AD 991	Donald Scragg (ed.), *The Battle of Maldon, AD 991* (Oxford: Basil Blackwell, 1991)

Political Writings	Andrew Rabin, *The Political Writings of Archbishop Wulfstan of York* (Manchester: Manchester University Press, 2015)
Roach, *Æthelred the Unready*	Levi Roach, *Æthelred the Unready* (New Haven, CT, and London: Yale University Press, 2016)
S	P. H. Sawyer, *Anglo-Saxon Charters: An Annotated List and Bibliography*, revised by S. E. Kelly and R. Rushforth as the 'Electronic Sawyer' (www.esawyer.org.uk). Charters are cited by their 'Sawyer' or 'S' number
Wiley Blackwell Encyclopedia	*Wiley Blackwell Encyclopedia of Anglo-Saxon England*, ed. Michael Lapidge et al. (Oxford: Wiley-Blackwell, 2014)
Williams	Ann Williams, *Æthelred the Unready: The Ill-Counselled King* (London: Hambledon Continuum, 2003)
WM	*William of Malmesbury: Gesta Regum Anglorum, The History of the English Kings*, vol. 1, ed. R. A. B. Mynors, R. M. Thomson and M. Winterbottom (Oxford: Oxford University Press, 1998)

Anglo-Saxon law codes (cited by abbreviated form, clause and subsection): Af. = Alfred; As. = Æthelstan; Atr. = Æthelred; Cn. = Cnut; Edg. = Edgar; Edm. = Edmund

INTRODUCTION

1. Simon Keynes, 'The Declining Reputation of Æthelred the Unready', in *Anglo-Saxon History: Basic Readings*, ed. David A. E. Pelteret (New York and London: Garland Publishing, 2000), p. 174.
2. Ibid., pp. 174-5.
3. Ibid., pp. 158-68; Simon Keynes, 'A Tale of Two Kings: Alfred the Great and Æthelred the Unready', *Transactions of the Royal Historical Society*, 5th Series, 36 (1986), pp. 201-4. For the different manuscripts of the *Chronicle*, see Michael Swanton, *The Anglo-Saxon Chronicle* (New York: Routledge, 1998), pp. xi-xxix. See also the 'Note on the Text' in the current volume.

I. MARTYRDOM MOST FOUL

1. Willams, pp. 11-15; Roach, *Æthelred the Unready*, pp. 68-77 and 168-74.
2. *ASC* 979 DE (correctly 978), trans. Swanton, p. 123.
3. The 'Sermon of the Wolf' survives in three versions of varying length, of which only the shortest explicitly refers to Æthelred's exile, although it is implied in the other two. The Old English texts are edited by Dorothy Bethurum, *The Homilies of Wulfstan* (Oxford: Oxford University Press, 1957), pp. 255-75. Michael Swanton provides a translation of the long version in his *Anglo-Saxon Prose* (London: Rowman and Littlefield, 1975), pp. 116-22. The relationship between the three versions and their dating are subjects of debate. Keynes argues that the longest version is the earliest of the three, but that all descend from a lost 'original' that Wulfstan preached in 1009 when the viking threat seemed most apocalyptic. The reference to Æthelred's exile was added when Wulfstan revised the sermon after

Swein's death. See Keynes, 'An Abbot', pp. 206–13. See also Roach, *Æthelred the Unready*, pp. 279–83.

4. Barbara Yorke, 'The Women in Edgar's Life', in *Edgar, King of the English*, pp. 143–57.

5. *JW*, pp. 416–17; *WM*, pp. 258–60. The two accounts are almost certainly related.

6. S 725, 771, 779, 794, 795, 801, 805 and 806.

7. Janet Nelson, 'The Second English *Ordo*', in her *Politics and Ritual in Early Medieval Europe* (London: Hambledon Press, 1986), p. 372.

8. Pauline Stafford, *Queen Emma and Queen Edith: Queenship and Women's Power in Eleventh-Century England* (Oxford: Blackwell, 1997), p. 164.

9. Andrew Rabin, 'Female Advocacy and Royal Protection in Tenth-Century England: The Legal Career of Queen Ælfthryth', *Speculum*, 84:2 (2009), pp. 273–88.

10. S 745.

11. *Regularis Concordia Anglicae Nationis Monachorum Sanctimonialiumque*, ed. and trans. Thomas Symons (London: Thomas Nelson and Sons, 1953), p. 2. Edgar's decision to entrust the protection of nuns to Ælfthryth is in Bishop Æthelwold's account of Edgar's establishment of monasteries. See *EHD*, p. 848.

12. Barbara Yorke, 'Æthelwold and the Politics of the Tenth Century', in her *Bishop Æthelwold: His Career and Influence* (Woodbridge: Boydell Press, 1988), pp. 82–4.

13. S 745.

14. D. J. V. Fisher, 'The Anti-Monastic Reaction in Edward the Martyr's Reign', *Cambridge History Journal*, 10 (1952), p. 260; *Diplomas*, p. 166.

15. Williams, p. 9.

16. Rabin, 'Legal Career of Queen Ælfthryth', pp. 279–80.

17. King Æthelstan established twelve as the threshold for legal adulthood (II As. 1, 1.1. Cf. II Cn. 21).

18. Ecclesiastes 10:16.

19. *ASC* 975 ADE.

20. Fisher, 'Anti-Monastic Reaction', pp. 254–70; Simon Keynes, 'Edgar, *Rex Admirabilis*', in *Edgar, King of the English*, pp. 54–6.

21. *Life of St Oswald*, pp. 136–43; *EHD*, pp. 841–3.

22. *Life of St Oswald*, pp. 136–8; *EHD*, p. 841.

23. Michael Lapidge, 'Byrhtferth and Oswald', in *St Oswald of Worcester: Life and Influence*, ed. Nicholas Brooks and Catherine Cubitt (London and New York: Leicester University Press, 1996), pp. 79–80.

24. Af. 4; III Edg. 7.3; II Cn. 64.

25. *ASC* 979 E (correctly 978), trans. Swanton, p. 123.

26. *Life of St Oswald*, pp. 142–3; *EHD*, pp. 839–49.

27. The earliest account to implicate Ælfthryth in the murder is the *Passio Sancti Eadward Regis et Martyris*, composed probably by Goscelin of Saint-Bertin in the 1070s. See C. F. Fell (ed. and trans), *Edward, King and Martyr*, Leeds Texts and Monographs (Leeds: University of Leeds, 1971), pp. xiv–xx.

28. Henry of Huntingdon, *Historia Anglorum*, ed. and trans. Diana Greenway (Oxford: Oxford University Press), pp. 324–5 and n. 186.

29. *Liber Eliensis: A History from the Seventh Century to the Twelfth, Compiled by a Monk of Ely in the Twelfth Century*, trans. Janet Fairweather (Woodbridge: Boydell Press, 2005), pp. 153–4.

30. *ASC* 979 CE. Cf. *Life of St Oswald*, pp. 154–5; *EHD*, p. 843.
31. S 937. See Roach, *Æthelred the Unready*, pp. 70–71.
32. Fell (ed. and trans.), *Edward, King and Martyr*, pp. 6–7.
33. *EHD*, p. 857. See Catherine Cubitt, 'Sites and Sanctity: Revising the Cult of Murdered and Martyred Anglo-Saxon Royal Saints', *Early Medieval Europe*, 9 (2000), p. 83.
34. Nicole Marafioti, *The King's Body: Burial and Succession in Late Anglo-Saxon England* (Toronto: University of Toronto Press, 2014), pp. 163–76.
35. Susan Ridyard, *The Royal Saints of Anglo-Saxon England* (Cambridge: Cambridge University Press, 1988), pp. 69–71; Barbara Yorke, *Nunneries and the Anglo-Saxon Royal Houses* (London: Continuum, 2003), pp. 171–2; Marafioti, *The King's Body*, pp. 181–2.
36. *Wiley Blackwell Encyclopedia*, 'Kingston-upon-Thames' (S. Keynes).
37. *Life of St Oswald*, pp. 108 and 109; Roach, *Æthelred the Unready*, pp. 82–4.
38. Digital edition of the Old English coronation oath (*Promissio Regis*), ed. and trans. Mary Clayton, 'Early English Laws' website (http://www.earlyenglishlaws. ac.uk/laws/texts/sacr-cor/view/#edition,1/translation,1); *Laws*, pp. 4–3. See Pauline Stafford, 'The Laws of Cnut and the History of Anglo-Saxon Royal Promises', *ASE*, 10 (1981), pp. 185–6.

2. THE YEARS OF YOUTHFUL
IGNORANCE

1. *Diplomas*, pp. 174–5.
2. Bishop Æthelwold: S 835, where the donation to the Old Minster, Winchester, is described as 'first fruits' following the 'royal consecration'. Ealdorman Ælfhere: S 834, 'to my . . . faithful ealdorman and blood relation'.
3. Levi Roach, 'Hosting the King: Hospitality and the Royal *Iter* in Tenth-Century England', *Journal of Medieval History*, 37 (2011), pp. 34–46.
4. David Hill, *An Atlas of Anglo-Saxon England* (Toronto: University of Toronto Press, 1981), nos. 156–63 and 167–9.
5. *Annales Cambriae*, entry for 983, cited in T. M. Charles-Edwards, *Wales and the Britons, 350–1064* (Oxford: Oxford University Press, 2013), pp. 548–9.
6. Roach, *Æthelred the Unready*, p. 87.
7. S 896. Ælfric's expulsion from England is recorded in *ASC* 985 CDE.
8. Roach, *Æthelred the Unready*, p. 106.
9. Williams, p. 66.
10. S 883; I Atr. 4.2.
11. *Diplomas*, pp. 183–4.
12. *ASC* 986 CDE.
13. Bernard Scholz, 'Sulcard of Westminster: "Prologus de Construccione Westmonesterii"', *Traditio*, 20 (1964), pp. 89–90.
14. R. H. M. Dolley, 'Æthelred's Rochester Ravaging of 986: An Intriguing Numismatic Sidelight', *Spinks Numismatics Circular*, 75 (1967), pp. 33–4.
15. *Diplomas*, pp. 178–9; Williams, pp. 26–8.
16. See Catherine Cubitt, 'Ælfric's Lay Patrons', in *A Companion to Ælfric*, ed. Hugh Magennis and Mary Swan (Leiden: Brill, 2009), pp. 165–85.

17. *Diplomas*, p. 187.
18. *ASC* 975 DE, trans. Swanton, p. 121.
19. *ASC* 980 C; 981 DE.
20. *ASC* 981 C, trans. Swanton, p. 124.
21. *ASC* 988 CDE.
22. *Life of St Oswald*, pp. 154-7.
23. S 1515.
24. Charles-Edwards, *Wales and the Britons*, pp. 539-46 and 550.
25. *ASC* 959 DE (emphasis added).
26. Else Roesdahl, *Viking Age Denmark* (London: British Museum, 1982), pp. 45-8 and 147-55, 172; Niels Lund, 'The Danish Empire and the End of the Viking Age', in *The Oxford Illustrated History of the Vikings*, ed. Peter Sawyer (Oxford: Oxford University Press, 1997), p. 161 and, more generally, pp. 158-66. For military developments in Scandinavia in the Second Viking Age, see Lavelle, pp. 52-64.
27. *ASC* 991 CDE; 993 A (correctly 991).

3. THE VIKING CHALLENGE

1. Alan Kennedy, 'Byrhtnoth's Obits and Twelfth-Century Accounts of the Battle of Maldon', in *Maldon, AD 991*, pp. 59-62.
2. *ASC* CDE 991, trans. Swanton, p. 127.
3. See Janet Bately, 'The *Anglo-Saxon Chronicle*', in *Maldon, AD 991*, pp. 46-7.
4. Swein's participation in the Maldon campaign may be inferred from a charter dated between 995 and 999 (S 939). The Chronicler (991) and the *Maldon* poet (line 129) both identify the vikings at Maldon as Danes, which, if accurate, would support the presence of Swein but not Olaf.
5. Niels Lund, 'The Armies of Swein Forkbeard and Cnut: *leding* or *lith*?', *ASE*, 15 (1986), pp. 105-18; Niels Lund, 'Danish Military Organisation', in *The Battle of Maldon: Fiction and Fact*, ed. Janet Cooper (London: Hambledon Press, 1993), pp. 109-26.
6. Twenty-eight runestones in Sweden refer to vikings who campaigned in England. For texts and translations, see 'England runestones' Wikipedia entry (https://en.wikipedia.org/wiki/England_runestones).
7. Judith Jesch, *Ships and Men in the Late Viking Age: The Vocabulary of Runic Inscriptions and Skaldic Verse* (Woodbridge: Boydell & Brewer, 2001), pp. 44-67; Kim Hjardar and Vegard Vike, *Vikings at War* (Oxford and Philadelphia: Casemate, 2016), p. 17.
8. Byrhtnoth and wife are named as beneficiaries in the will of his father-in-law Ealdorman Ælfgar (S 1483), which was drawn up at least forty years before the battle.
9. See R. Abels, 'English Tactics, Strategy and Military Organization in the Late Tenth Century', in *Maldon, AD 991*, p. 148.
10. W. A. Samouce, 'General Byrhtnoth', *Journal of English and Germanic Philology*, 62 (1963), p. 131. See also I. J. Kirby, 'In Defence of Byrhtnoth', *Florilegium*, 11 (1992), pp. 53-60.
11. M. Lapidge, 'Life of St Oswald', in *Maldon, AD 991*, p. 55.
12. *ASC* 948 CDE, when a force from York fell upon the rearguard of King Eadred's army as they were marching south, after having ravaged Northumbria.
13. *ASC* 992 CDE: *ahwaer utene* means literally 'somewhere outside/abroad', which Swanton reasonably interprets as taking place in the estuary. See Swanton, p. 127, n. 8.

14. *ASC* 992 CDE, trans. Swanton, p. 127.

15. *ASC* 993 CDE. He is probably the royal thegn Ælfgar who appears prominently in the witness lists to Æthelred's charters between 982 and 990, and who was a royal reeve. See *Diplomas*, pp. 184–5.

16. Discussed in Stephen Baxter, *The Lords of Mercia: Lordship and Power in Late Anglo-Saxon England* (Oxford: Oxford University Press, 2008), pp. 81–4.

17. Rory Naismith, *European Medieval Coinage*, vol. 8: *Britain and Ireland c.400–1066* (Cambridge: Cambridge University Press, 2017), pp. 231–2 and 265–6.

18. The text is edited and discussed by W. Braekman, 'Wyrdwriteras: An Unpublished Ælfrician Text in Hatton 115', *Revue belge de philologie et d'histoire*, 44 (1966), pp. 959–70.

19. V Atr. 28, 28.1; VI Atr. 35.

20. V Atr. 35.

21. *The Battle of Maldon*, ed. and trans. Donald Scragg, in *Maldon, AD 991*, pp. 18–31.

22. III Edm. 1.

23. *JW*, pp. 482–3.

24. 'Eall here bið hwæt þonne lateow byþ hwæt', quoted in Thomas Hill, '"When the Leader is Brave . . .": An Old English Proverb and its Vernacular Context', *Anglia: Zeitschrift für englische Philologie*, 119 (2001), p. 232.

25. *ASC* 1003 CDE.

26. *EHD*, p. 796.

27. *ASC* 993 CDE; *JW*, pp. 442–3.

28. *Encomium Emmae*, ed. and trans. Alistair Campbell with a supplementary introduction by Simon Keynes (Cambridge: Cambridge University Press, 1998), pp. 32–3. The Encomiast, a Flemish monk writing around 1041–2, describes Eadric (pp. 24–5) as 'a man skilful in counsel but treacherous in guile'. Eadric's nickname, meaning 'the acquisitor', first appears in *Hemming's Cartulary*, a late eleventh-century collection of the charters and deeds of the cathedral chapter of Worcester placed into historical context by the monk Hemming to defend that church's legal right to its estates. See *Hemingi Chartularium Ecclesiae Wigorniensis*, ed. Thomas Hearne (Oxford: 1723), pp. 280–81.

29. See R. Abels, 'Cowardice and Duty in Anglo-Saxon England', *Journal of Medieval Military History*, 6 (2006), pp. 29–48.

30. C. R. Hart, *The Early Charters of Northern England and the North Midlands* (Leicester: Leicester University Press, 1975), pp. 335 and 336–7; Williams, p. 181, n. 14; *Attestations*, Table LXIII.

31. Niels Lund, 'The Danish Perspective', in *Maldon, AD 991*, pp. 133–49.

32. *ASC* 994 CDE. The Chronicler has the attack begin on the feast of the Nativity of Saint Mary, i.e. 8 September. Events in this annal are reported under 993 in the A manuscript. The discrepancy may have been due to the use of different commencement days for the year, CDE employing 1 September, and A either Christmas or 1 January. All three were at that time possible New Year's days. See Ian Howard, *Swein Forkbeard's Invasions and the Danish Conquest of England, 991–1017* (Woodbridge: Boydell & Brewer, 2003), pp. 42–3.

33. *ASC* 994 CDE, trans. Swanton, p. 129; II Atr. 1.

34. Niels Lund, 'Peace and Non-Peace in the Viking Age Ottar in Biarmaland, the Rus in Byzantium, and Danes and Norwegians in England', in *Proceedings of the Tenth Viking Congress*, ed. J. E. Knirk (Oslo: Universitetets Oldsaksamling, 1987), pp. 265–6.

35. *ASC* 994 CDE.

36. *II Æthelred*, quoted in Simon Keynes, 'The Historical Context of the Battle of Maldon', in *Maldon, AD 991*, p. 106; *Laws*, p. 57.

37. Lund, 'Peace and Non-Peace', pp. 264–8. See also R. Abels, 'Household Men, Mercenaries and Vikings in Anglo-Saxon England', in *Mercenaries and Paid Men: The Mercenary Identity in the Middle Ages*, ed. John Gillingham (Leiden: Brill, 2008), pp. 155–7.

38. II Atr. 6.1. Norse landowners are implied by II Atr. 7, which protects a 'shipman' (*sceithman*) against English cattle-rustlers, and an appendix to the treaty concerned with property disputes and vouching to warranty (*team*).

39. Keynes suggests that Pallig received his 'great gifts, in estates and gold and silver' in connection with this treaty. Keynes, 'The Vikings in England: *c*.790–1016', in Sawyer (ed.), *Oxford Illustrated History of the Vikings*, p. 77.

40. *ASC* 993 A (correctly 991); 994 CDE.

41. Lesley Abrams, 'The Anglo-Saxons and the Christianization of Scandinavia', *ASE*, 24 (1995), pp. 220–23. Olaf promoted Christianity aggressively in pagan Norway. See also Lund, 'Danish Perspective', pp. 138–40; Theodore M. Andersson, 'The Viking Policy of Ethelred the Unready', *Scandinavian Studies*, 99 (1987), pp. 284–95.

42. *ASC* 994, trans. Swanton, p. 129.

43. *ASC* 999 CDE, trans. Swanton, p. 133.

44. Simon Keynes, 'Conspectus of Edgar's Charters', in *Edgar, King of the English*, pp. 60–80. Æthelred is styled *rex totius insule*, 'king of the whole island', in a charter (S 898) issued in the year following the campaign. Andreas Lemke, 'Voices from the Reign of Æthelred II', in *Von Æthelred zum Mann im Mond: Forschungsarbeiten aus der englischen Mediävistik*, ed. Janna Müller and Frauke Reitemeier (Göttingen: Universitätsverlag Göttingen, 2010), pp. 21–2.

45. The battle at Dean is reported only in the A manuscript of the *Anglo-Saxon Chronicle*. The battle probably drew the attention of the monks of the Old Minster, Winchester, because one of the casualties was the son of a bishop of Winchester. The contemporary account in A tellingly lacks the pessimism and criticisms that suffuse the entry for 1001 in CDE. Keynes, 'A Tale of Two Kings', p. 202.

46. *ASC* 1001 A, trans. Swanton, p. 132.

47. *ASC* 1002 CDE.

48. *Memorials of St Dunstan*, ed. W. Stubbs (London: Longman, 1874), pp. 397–8, trans. *EHD*, pp. 82–3.

49. S 909, in which she is said to have been 'consecrated to the royal bed'. See Stafford, *Queen Emma and Queen Edith*, pp. 174–5.

50. *Diplomas*, p. 210, n. 2003.

51. S 904. Pauline Stafford, 'Queens, Nunneries and Reforming Churchmen: Gender, Religious Status and Reform in Tenth- and Eleventh-Century England', *Past and Present*, 163 (1999), pp. 4 and 19.

52. Pauline Stafford suggests that the nuns of Wherwell sought the privilege as protection against the new queen: 'Queens, Nunneries', pp. 25–7.

53. Exodus 20:12, in Roach, *Æthelred the Unready*, pp. 189–90.

54. *ASC* 1001 A.

55. *ASC* 1002 CDE, trans. Swanton, p. 135.

56. S 909; *EHD*, pp. 545–6.

57. Kings Alfred and Æthelstan had both issued legislation assuring church sanctuary (*cyricgrið*), as would Æthelred himself six years after the burning of St

Frideswide's church, probably at the urging of Wulfstan. See Af. 2.1, 5.4, 42.2; IV As. 6; VI Atr. 14; VIII Atr. 1.1. Wulfstan's views on the inviolability of church sanctuary are most fully articulated in the texts 'Grið' and 'Nor Grið', in *Political Writings*, pp. 76–84.

58. See Roach, *Æthelred the Unready*, p. 196. The parable of the cockle among the wheat was used to countenance the burning of heretics during the High Middle Ages (Levi Roach, personal communiqué). See also Ann Williams, '"Cockles Amongst the Wheat": Danes and English in the West Midlands in the First Half of the Eleventh century', *Midland History*, 11 (1986), pp. 1–22.

59. Sean Wallis (ed.), *The Oxford Henge and Late Saxon Massacre; with Medieval and Late Occupation at St John's College, Oxford* (Reading: Thames Valley Archaeological Services, 2014), pp. 37–158. A second mass grave of slain vikings was discovered in 2009 on Ridgeway Hill between Dorchester and Weymouth in Dorset. This one contained the disarticulated skeletons of fifty-four men (but only fifty-one skulls) who had been violently killed. Chemical analysis and radio-carbon dating determined that they too were Scandinavian males of fighting age killed probably sometime during the reign of Æthelred. Given the location of the burial pit, the dead may have been vikings captured during a raid or a company of mercenaries billeted in either Dorchester or Portland. See Louise Loe, Angela Boyle, Helen Webb, David Score, *'Given to the Ground': A Viking Age Mass Grave on Ridgeway Hill, Weymouth* (Dorchester: Dorset Natural History and Archaeological Society, 2014).

60. See Williams, pp. 53–4; Roach, *Æthelred the Unready*, pp. 192–200. Ryan Lavelle suggests that the victims were Scandinavian merchants. See Lavelle, p. 100.

61. *WM*, pp. 300–301; Williams, p. 54.

62. The Danes' praise of the East Anglians' 'hand-play' is in the entry for 1004 in manuscripts C and D but not E. See Swanton, p. 136, n. 1.

63. *ASC* 1005 CDE, trans. Swanton, p. 136.

4. THE POLITICS OF REPENTANCE

1. *Diplomas*, pp. 186–208.

2. Æthelstan credits Ælfthryth in his will (S 1503) with having raised him (*me affede*).

3. For Ælfgar, see S 861 and 918; for Æthelsige, see S 864 and 893. *Diplomas*, pp. 182–5; *Attestations*, Table LXIII.

4. S 893. See comments in Williams, pp. 26–7.

5. S 876. See Roach, *Æthelred the Unready*, pp. 136–52.

6. *Diplomas*, p. 177.

7. Abingdon: S 876 and 937; Old Minster, Winchester: S 891; Rochester: S 885 and 893.

8. The translation is by Catherine Cubitt in her 'The Politics of Remorse: Penance and Royal Piety in the Reign of Æthelred the Unready', *Historical Research*, 85 (2012), p. 182, n. 20.

9. Ibid., p. 191.

10. Levi Roach, 'Penitential Discourse in the Diplomas of King Æthelred "the Unready"', *The Journal of Ecclesiastical History*, 64 (2013), pp. 258–76; Roach, *Æthelred the Unready*, pp. 136–52.

11. S 876 and 937.
12. The Junius and *Beowulf* manuscripts, and perhaps the *Vercelli Book*, can be dated to Æthelred's reign.
13. See M. Lapidge's introduction in *Life of St Oswald*, pp. xv–lxiv.
14. *The Homilies of the Anglo-Saxon Church: The First Part, Containing the Sermones Catholici or the Homilies of Ælfric*, 2 vols, ed. and trans. Benjamin Thorpe (1844; reprinted Cambridge: Cambridge University Press, 2013), I, pp. 3–8.
15. Mary Clayton, 'Ælfric and Æthelred', in *Essays on Anglo-Saxon and Related Themes in Memory of Lynne Grundy*, ed. J. Roberts and J. Nelson (Woodbridge: Boydell & Brewer, 2000), pp. 65–88.
16. *Making of English Law*, pp. 451–4; *Political Writings*, pp. 40–41.
17. *The Institutes of Polity*, chs 3–5, in *Political Writings*, pp. 105–8.
18. M. K. Lawson, 'Archbishop Wulfstan and the Homiletic Element in the Law Codes of Æthelred II and Cnut', *EHR*, 107 (1992), pp. 565–86; *Making of English Law*, pp. 449–65.
19. S 899. See Roach, *Æthelred the Unready*, pp. 172–3.
20. See, for example, the preface to *IV Edgar*.
21. Clayton, 'Ælfric and Æthelred', p. 81.
22. Pseudo-Cyprianus, *De XII Abusivis Saeculi*, ed. S. Hellmann, in *Texte und Untersuchungen zur Geschichte der altchristlichen Literatur*, Reihe 3, Band 4, Heft 1 (Leipzig: Hinrichs, 1909), p. 52.
23. Translated in Clayton, 'Ælfric and Æthelred', p. 80, n. 47.
24. See Mary Clayton, '*De Duodecim Abusiuis*, Lordship and Kingship in Anglo-Saxon England', in S. McWilliams (ed.), *Saints and Scholars: New Perspectives on Anglo-Saxon Literature and Culture* (Woodbridge: Boydell & Brewer, 2012), pp. 141–63.
25. *Councils and Synods with Other Documents Relating to the English Church: A.D. 871–1204*, vol. 1, ed. D. Whitelock, M. Brett and C. Brooke (Oxford: Oxford University Press, 1981), pp. 224–6; quoted in Keynes, 'An Abbot', p. 171.
26. Keynes, 'An Abbot', pp. 179–89.

5. LAW AND (DIS)ORDER

1. See, for example, James Campbell, *The Anglo-Saxon State* (London and New York: Hambledon Press, 2000); Patrick Wormald, 'Giving God and King their Due' (1997), in his *Legal Culture in the Early Medieval West: Law as Text, Image and Experience* (London: Hambledon Press, 1999), pp. 333–55.
2. See Naismith, *European Medieval Coinage*, pp. 211–68.
3. III Atr. 8.1; V Atr. 32.1. Discussed by Daniel Gorman, 'Mutilation and Spectacle in Anglo-Saxon Legislation', in *Capital and Corporal Punishment in Anglo-Saxon England*, ed. J. P. Gates and N. Marafioti (Woodbridge: Boydell, 2014), pp. 149–64.
4. III Atr. 16; IV Atr. 5, 5.3, 7.1, 7.3.
5. Elina Screen, 'Anglo-Saxon Law and Numismatics: A Reassessment in Light of Patrick Wormald's *The Making of English Law*', *British Numismatics Society*, 77 (2007), pp. 161–2.
6. Robin Fleming, *Britain after Rome: The Fall and Rise, 400–1070* (London: Allen Lane, 2010), pp. 290–317.

7. The reliability of the Chronicler's escalating figures for the payment of tribute is debated by John Gillingham and M. K. Lawson in vols 104 and 105 (1989 and 1990) in the *EHR*. Lawson effectively answers Gillingham's objections.

8. The monk Hemming, writing in the late eleventh century, claims that the church of Worcester had lost much of its gold and silver plate to pay 'huge and unbearable' royal taxes and tribute during the reign of Æthelred. *Hemingi Chartularium*, p. 248, quoted in Williams, pp. 229–30, n. 15.

9. Naismith, *European Medieval Coinage*, pp. 224 and 261–9.

10. Screen, 'Anglo-Saxon Law and Numismatics', pp. 152, 156 and 157.

11. Simon Keynes and Rory Naismith, 'The *Agnus Dei* Pennies of King Æthelred the Unready', *ASE*, 40 (2012), pp. 175–223.

12. *Wiley Blackwell Encyclopedia*, 'Council, King's' (B. A. E. Yorke).

13. For pledges of love and loyalty to kings, see III Edm. 1; V Atr. 35; VI Atr. 1; VIII Atr. 44.1; I Cn. 1, 20.

14. *Wiley-Blackwell Encyclopedia*, 'Trinoda Necessitas' (R. Abels).

15. The first reference to hundred courts is the 'Hundred Ordinance', traditionally called *I Edgar*. See *Making of English Law*, pp. 378–9.

16. I Edg. 1; III Edg. 5.

17. II As. 23; 'Decree concerning hot iron and water', in F. L. Attenborough (ed. and trans.), *The Laws of the Earliest English Kings* (Cambridge: Cambridge University Press, 1922), pp. 140–41 and 170–71. For further discussion, see Sarah Larratt Keefer, '*Ðonne se Cirlisca Men Ordales Weddigeð*: The Anglo-Saxon Lay Ordeal', in *Early Medieval Studies in Memory of Patrick Wormald*, ed. S. Baxter et al. (Farnham: Ashgate, 2009), pp. 353–67.

18. Tom Lambert, *Law and Order in Anglo-Saxon England* (Oxford: Oxford University Press, 2017), pp. 106–7 and 163–201.

19. III Edg. 6; IV Edg. 3; I Atr. 1.

20. II Cn. 20.

21. II As. 20, discussed in Lambert, *Law and Order*, pp. 153–6.

22. *Making of English Law*, pp. 320–45. Several 'non-official' legal texts, most if not all written by Archbishop Wulfstan, also date from Æthelred's reign. See also the 'Note on the Text' in this current volume.

23. The translation is Wormald's in his *Making of English Law*, pp. 336–7. For a sympathetic assessment of Æthelred's legislative legacy, see M. R. Rambaran-Olm, 'Trial by History's Jury: Examining II Æthelred's Legislative and Literary Legacy, AD 993–1006', *English Studies*, 95 (2014), pp. 777–802.

24. I Atr. Preface, 1, 1.10; III Atr. Preface, 4.

25. II Atr. 7, 8.

26. *Making of English Law*, p. 326.

27. 'Coronation Oath', trans. Clayton, 'Early English Laws' website; *Laws*, pp. 42–3. A main topic in Anglo-Saxon law codes is the detection and punishment of theft, especially of livestock, which even more than homicide was thought to be the main threat to public peace. Lambert, *Law and Order*, pp. 207–10. The oath to judge justly and with mercy is alluded to in V Atr. 3 and VI Atr. 53.

28. IV Edg. 1.5; VII Atr. 6.3; Cn. 1020 (Cnut's Proclamation of 1020), 11; II Cn. 69.

29. V Atr. 32.

30. *Institutes of Polity*, ch. 10, in *Political Writings*, p. 111.

31. Sean Miller (ed.), *Anglo-Saxon Charters IX: Charters of the New Minster, Winchester* (Oxford: Oxford University Press, 2001), no. 31, pp. 144–8, and A. G.

Robertson (ed.), *Anglo-Saxon Charters* (Cambridge: Cambridge University Press, 1956), no. 63, pp. 128–9; *EHD*, pp. 531–2.

32. R. Abels, '"The crimes by which Wulfbald ruined himself with his lord": The Limits of State Action in Late Anglo-Saxon England', *Reading Medieval Studies*, 40 (2014; special issue: *Law's Dominion in the Middle Ages: Essays for Paul Hyams*, ed. David Postles), pp. 42–53.

33. Simon Keynes, 'Crime and Punishment in the Reign of Æthelred the Unready', in *People and Places in Northern Europe 500–1600: Essays in Honour of Peter Hayes Sawyer*, ed. I. Wood and N. Lund (Woodbridge: Boydell & Brewer, 1991), pp. 76–7. I tend to concur with Dorothy Whitelock (*EHD*, p. 47) that the narratives are included as justifications of Æthelred's legal title to the properties. For alternative explanations, see Keynes, 'Crime and Punishment', p. 77.

34. I Edg. 3.1.

35. Keynes, 'Crime and Punishment', p. 79. See, for example, IV As. 3, concerning men of kin groups so powerful that they could break the law and harbour criminals with impunity.

36. Andrew Rabin, 'Capital Punishment and the Anglo-Saxon Judicial Apparatus: A Maximum View?', in *Capital and Corporal Punishment*, ed. Gates and Marafioti, pp. 181–200.

37. S 883.

38. I Atr. 4.2., for the prohibition of Christian burial for those who abet thieves.

6. LOSING THE KINGDOM

1. Swanton (trans.), *Anglo-Saxon Prose*, pp. 118, 120.
2. *ASC* 1014 CDE, trans. Swanton, p. 145.
3. *Attestations*, Tables LX (a and b) and LXIII (pp. 2–3).
4. *Diplomas*, pp. 209–13.
5. S 937 (*EHD*, pp. 537–9); *ASC* 1006; *JW*, pp. 456–7.
6. *JW*, pp. 456–9. Cf. *ASC* 1006 CDE.
7. *Diplomas*, pp. 189, 211–13; Williams, pp. 70–72.
8. For King Edgar's edict substituting comprehensive mutilation for execution, see 'The Translations and Miracles of St Swithun', cited and translated in *Making of English Law*, p. 125. II Cn. 30.5, *Laws*, pp. 190–91, provides the rationale.
9. C. Insley, 'Politics, Conflict and Kinship in Early Eleventh-Century Mercia', *Midland History*, 25 (2000), pp. 28–35.
10. S 887, 893, 896 and 910.
11. S 901.
12. Evidence for the high status of the family comes from *ASC* 943 D, which mentions the capture of their mother Wulfrun by Olaf Sihtricson in a raid on Mercia. For the families of Ælfhelm and Eadric, see Williams, pp. 33–5 and 70–71.
13. *Attestations*, Table LXII (2).
14. *ASC* 1006 CDE; Lavelle, pp. 113–16.
15. *ASC* 1008 CE. D has 300 hides. G. N. Garmonsway, noting the odd phrasing of CE and the possibility of a missing word, makes the attractive suggestion that text originally read: 'a large ship from every three hundred hides and *a cutter* from every ten hides' (emphasis added). *The Anglo-Saxon Chronicle* (London: J. M. Dent & Sons, 1953), p. 138. For ship-sokes in the reign of Edgar, see F. E.

Harmer, *Anglo-Saxon Writs* (Manchester: Manchester University Press, 1952), pp. 266–9.

16. This finds support in both the poem *The Battle of Maldon* and in the heriots (a death tax of weapons) appearing in wills. See Nicholas Brooks, 'Weapons and Armour', in *Maldon, AD 991*, pp. 215–17.

17. *ASC* 1009 CDE.

18. D. Hill, 'Trends in the Development of Towns in the Reign of Ethelred II', in *Ethelred the Unready: Papers from the Millenary Conference*, ed. D. Hill, British Archaeological Reports, 59 (London: BAR Publishing, 1978), pp. 214–26; L. Alcock, *Cadbury Castle, Somerset: The Early Medieval Archaeology* (Cardiff: University of Wales Press, 1995), pp. 165–9; Jeremy Haslam, 'Daws Castle, Somerset, and Civil Defence Measures in Southern and Midland England in the Ninth to Eleventh Centuries', *Archaeological Journal*, 168 (2011), pp. 195–226.

19. J. Baker and S. Brookes, *Beyond the Burghal Hidage* (Leiden: Brill, 2013), pp. 82–5. Haslam argues that in some cases the replacement of timber by stone defences dates to Alfred's reign. See 'Daws Castle', pp. 210–17.

20. *Rectitudines Singularum Personarum*, 'Thegn's Law', trans. *EHD*, p. 813.

21. Baker and Brookes, *Beyond the Burghal Hidage*, pp. 355–9 and 398–9.

22. *ASC* 1009 CDE.

23. Williams, pp. 115–17.

24. *ASC* 1009 CDE.

25. Ibid.

26. IV Edg., Preface, 1.

27. The Enham Code is preserved in two forms, *V* and *VI Æthelred*. The latter, of which there are both Old English and Latin versions, may represent revisions by Archbishop Wulfstan in preparation for the legislation he drafted for Cnut. See *Making English Law*, pp. 332–5.

28. Keynes, 'An Abbot', pp. 151–220.

29. VII Atr. 1.

30. Keynes and Naismith, '*Agnus Dei* Pennies'.

31. *ASC* 1011 CDE.

32. Ibid., and *JW*, pp. 468–70. The *Anglo-Saxon Chronicle* also reports the seizure of Ælfweard the king's reeve, Abbess Leofrun of Minster in Thanet, Bishop Godwine of Rochester, 'and all ordained people, both men and women' in Canterbury, although apparently only the archbishop was held for ransom. See Swanton, p. 141.

33. Although Archbishop Ælfheah was treated as a martyr by the Chronicler and subsequent medieval writers, his killing probably had little to do with religion. Christian conversion of Scandinavia, in particular Denmark, was well under way by the early eleventh century, and many of those in Thorkell's 'raiding army', perhaps even Thorkell himself, were Christians. See Anders Winroth, *The Conversion of Scandinavia: Vikings, Merchants, and Missionaries in the Remaking of Northern Europe* (New Haven, CT: Yale University Press, 2011). Ryan Lavelle points out that Archbishop Ælfheah's 'martyrdom' was an exceptional event and that the vikings who raided Æthelred's kingdom did not deliberately target churches or churchmen. See Lavelle, pp. 93–4. None the less, the brutal killing of an archbishop reinforced stereotypes inherited from the viking wars of the ninth century about viking savagery and their association with paganism. See Roach, *Æthelred the Unready*, pp. 264–6.

34. *ASC* 1012.

35. *Diplomas*, p. 267.

36. M. Godden, 'Apocalypse and Invasion in Late Anglo-Saxon England', in *From Anglo-Saxon to Early Middle English: Studies Presented to E. G. Stanley*, ed. M. Godden et al. (Oxford: Oxford University Press, 1994), p. 144; J. Wilcox, 'Wulfstan's *Sermo Lupi ad Anglos* as Political Performance: 16 February 1014 and Beyond', in *Wulfstan, Archbishop of York*, ed. M. Townend (Turnhout: Brepols, 2004), pp. 380–81.

37. For the 'Sermon of the Wolf', see ch. 1, n. 3, above.

38. *ASC* 1014 CDE, trans. Swanton, p. 214.

39. II Cn. 69.

40. S 882, S 933. Æthelred himself sold estates to raise money to pay tribute. S 943.

41. Insley, 'Politics, Power', pp. 30 and 31.

42. *ASC* 1015 CDE.

43. Æthelstan's will (S 1503; *EHD*, pp. 549–50), drawn up probably in 1014 just before his death, connects Edmund, Ulfcytel, Sigeferth, Morcar and Godwine, son of Wulfnoth. It is tempting to see the beneficiaries of the will as comprising the court faction opposed to Eadric. The close relationship between Æthelstan and Edmund is attested by his bequest to his brother of a sword that had belonged to King Offa, as well as extensive lands. Æthelstan also left a sword and land to his younger brother Edmund. It is perhaps significant that he left nothing to his young half-brothers, Edward and Alfred.

44. *ASC* 1016 C; *JW*, pp. 146–7.

EPILOGUE AND CONCLUSION

1. The site of the battle is uncertain. 'Assandun' has been traditionally identified with Ashingdon in south-east Essex, but a strong case has been made for the village of Ashdon, near the Essex/Cambridgeshire border. See Warwick Rodwell, 'The Battle of *Assandun* and its Memorial Church: A Reappraisal', in *The Battle of Maldon: Fiction and Fact*, pp. 127–58, and C. R. Hart, *The Danelaw* (London: Hambledon Press, 1992), pp. 553–65.

2. *ASC* 1016 CDE. The *Encomium Emmae Reginae* (I.15) confirms that Eadric fled the battlefield and says that he afterwards 'pretended' to have done so to ensure the victory for Cnut. See *Encomium*, p. 31.

3. *ASC* 1009 CDE, trans. Swanton, p. 141.

Further Reading

There are at present three good full-length biographies of King Æthelred II with complementary strengths. Ryan Lavelle's *Æthelred II: King of the English 978–1016* (Stroud: Tempus, 2002) is probably the best of the three in dealing with military actions and developments in Scandinavia. Ann Williams, *Æthelred the Unready: The Ill-Counselled King* (New York and London: Hambledon Continuum, 2003), does a masterful job analysing the charter evidence to reconstruct aristocratic familial and political connections. Levi Roach, *Æthelred the Unready* (New Haven, CT: Yale University Press, 2016), is the most ambitious of the three. Roach attempts the daunting task of uncovering something of the inner man from the few primary sources we have from Æthelred's reign. He contends that Æthelred, sharing the world view of the Benedictine reformers, sincerely believed that the misfortunes that befell his realm were divine punishment for his and his people's sins, and acted upon those beliefs. Roach also is to be commended for placing Æthelred into a broader European perspective.

All three biographies draw upon the work of Simon Keynes. Keynes is without a doubt the doyen of Æthelredian studies. His book *The Diplomas of King Æthelred the Unready, 978–1016* (Cambridge: Cambridge University Press, 1980) and the many articles and book chapters that followed have fundamentally reshaped the historiography of Æthelred's reign by challenging the traditional view as represented by Sir Frank Stenton's *Anglo-Saxon England*, 3rd edn (Oxford: Oxford University Press, 1971). Keynes has been most influential in his demonstration of the value of charters and coins as historical evidence. His overall assessment of Æthelred and his reign can be found in his entry on the king for the *Oxford Dictionary of National Biography* (https://

doi.org/10.1093/ref:odnb/8915). He reviews the challenges faced by would-be biographers of Æthelred in 'Re-Reading King Æthelred the Unready', his contribution to *Writing Medieval Biography, 750–1250: Essays in Honour of Professor Frank Barlow*, edited by D. Bates (Woodbridge: Boydell & Brewer, 2006).

The political roles played by Ælfthryth and Emma are examined by Pauline Stafford in *Queen Emma and Queen Edith: Queenship and Women's Power in Eleventh-Century England* (Oxford: Blackwell, 1997). Ælfthryth's activities as legal advocate and her gendered use of power are the focus of Andrew Rabin, 'Female Advocacy and Royal Protection in Tenth-Century England: The Legal Career of Queen Ælfthryth', *Speculum*, 84 (2009), pp. 273–88.

Pauline Stafford, *Unification and Conquest: A Political and Social History of England in the Tenth and Eleventh Centuries* (London: Edward Arnold, 1989), and George Molyneaux, *The Formation of the English Kingdom in the Tenth Century* (Oxford: Oxford University Press, 2015), consider the place of Æthelred's reign in the emergence of the kingdom of England. Stafford emphasizes the fragility of the unity of the realm. Molyneaux argues that the reigns of Edgar and Æthelred mark a watershed in the development and systematization of the administrative institutions of royal government. Æthelred's legislation is studied in detail by Patrick Wormald, *The Making of English Law: King Alfred to the Twelfth Century* (Oxford: Blackwell, 1999). M. R. Rambaran-Olm, 'Trial by History's Jury: Examining II Æthelred's Legislative and Literary Legacy, AD 993–1006', *English Studies*, 95 (2014), pp. 777–802, connects the legislative and literary accomplishments of the third quarter of Æthelred's reign. The best introductions to Æthelred's coinage are Rory Naismith's 'The Coinage of Æthelred II: A New Evaluation', *English Studies*, 97 (2016), pp. 117–39, and his *European Medieval Coinage*, vol. 8: *Britain and Ireland c.400–1066* (Cambridge: Cambridge University Press, 2017), ch. 10. For economic developments and material culture in late Anglo-Saxon England, see Robin Fleming, *Britain after Rome: The Fall and Rise, 400–1070* (London: Allen Lane, 2010).

Ryan Lavelle's *Alfred's Wars: Sources and Interpretations of Anglo-Saxon Warfare in the Viking Age* (Woodbridge: Boydell Press, 2010) covers the viking wars of Æthelred as well as those of Alfred. I explore the problems faced by English kings in making peace with vikings in 'Paying the Danegeld: Anglo-Saxon Peacemaking with the Vikings', in *War and Peace in Ancient and Medieval History*, edited by P. de Souza and J. France (Cambridge: Cambridge University Press, 2008), pp. 173–92. Kim Hjardar and Vegard Vike, *Vikings at War* (Oxford and Philadelphia: Casemate, 2016), provide a well-illustrated, comprehensive examination of all aspects of Scandinavian military history during the Viking Age. For the Battle of Maldon (and the poem), see the essays in Donald Scragg (ed.), *The Battle of Maldon, AD 991* (Oxford: Basil Blackwell, 1991), and Janet Cooper (ed.), *The Battle of Maldon: Fiction and Fact* (London: Hambledon Press, 1993). Ann Williams, '"Cockles Amongst the Wheat": Danes and English in the Western Midlands in the First Half of the Eleventh Century', *Midland History*, 11 (1986), pp. 1–22, considers the Saint Brice's Day Massacre in light of Danish settlement. For the mass burial of possible victims of the massacre discovered in Oxford, see A. M. Pollard et al., '"Sprouting Like Cockle Amongst the Wheat": The St Brice's Day Massacre and the Isotopic Analysis of Human Bones from St John's College, Oxford', *Oxford Journal of Archaeology*, 31 (2012), pp. 83–102. For other possible victims of the Saint Brice's Day Massacre, see Angela Boyle, 'Death on the Dorset Ridgeway: The Discovery and Execution of an Early Medieval Mass Burial', in Ryan Lavelle and Simon Roffey (eds,), *Danes in Wessex : The Scandinavian Impact on Southern England, c.800–c.1100* (Oxford: Oxbow Books, 2016).

M. Townend (ed.), *Wulfstan, Archbishop of York* (Turnhout: Brepols, 2004), and Hugh Magennis and Mary Swan (eds), *A Companion to Ælfric* (Leiden: Brill, 2009), are good introductions to the lives and works of the two most important churchmen of Æthelred's reign. The political writings of Wulfstan are edited and translated by Andrew Rabin in *The Political Writings of Archbishop Wulfstan of*

York (Manchester: Manchester University Press, 2015). Rabin's collection does not include the 'Sermon of the Wolf', but a translation can be found in Michael Swanton (ed.), *Anglo-Saxon Prose* (London: Rowman and Littlefield, 1975). Simon Keynes, 'An Abbot, an Archbishop and the Viking Raids of 1006–7 and 1009–12', *Anglo-Saxon England*, 36 (2007), pp. 151–220, explores how Wulfstan and Ælfric responded to the viking attacks. Mary Clayton, 'Ælfric and Æthelred', in *Essays on Anglo-Saxon and Related Themes in Memory of Lynne Grundy*, edited by J. Roberts and J. Nelson (Woodbridge: Boydell & Brewer, 2000), pp. 65–88, analyses Ælfric's allusions to and criticisms of Æthelred's kingship. Michael Lapidge (ed. and trans.), *Byrhtferth of Ramsey: The Lives of St Oswald and St Ecgwine* (Oxford: Oxford University Press, 2009), is the best introduction to the life and works of that eccentric writer.

The two translations of *The Anglo-Saxon Chronicle* that I prefer are by Michael Swanton (London: J. M. Dent, 1996) and Dorothy Whitelock (Norwich: Jarrold & Sons, 1961). Whitelock's is also in *English Historical Documents, Volume I: c.500–1042*, 2nd edn (London: Routledge, 1979), which has many of the key sources for Æthelred's reign. For the 'Æthelred–Cnut chronicle' in manuscripts CDE, see Alice Sheppard, *Families of the King: Writing Identity in the Anglo-Saxon Chronicle*, 2nd edn (Toronto: University of Toronto Press, 2004), and Courtney Konshuh, 'Anraed in their Unraed: The Æthelredian Annals (983–1016) and their Presentation of King and Advisors', *English Studies*, 97 (2016), pp. 140–62. Æthelred's law codes are translated by A. J. Robertson in *The Laws of the Kings of England from Edmund to Henry I* (Cambridge: Cambridge University Press, 1925). P. H. Sawyer, *Anglo-Saxon Charters: An Annotated List and Bibliography*, revised by S. E. Kelly and R. Rushforth (www.esawyer.org.uk), provides information about and texts of Æthelred's charters. The best source for maps relating to Æthelred's reign is David Hill, *An Atlas of Anglo-Saxon England* (Toronto: University of Toronto Press, 1981).

Picture Credits

1. A king with his witan, from the Old English Hexateuch, eleventh century. British Library, London. BL Cotton Claudius B. IV. f.59. (© British Library Board. All Rights Reserved/ Bridgeman Images)

2. The causeway to Northey Island, Essex. (National Trust Photographic Library/James Dobson/Bridgeman Images)

3. The Sea Stallion from Glendalough, a modern reconstruction of the longship Skuldelev 2. (© Viking Ship Museum, Roskilde)

4. Reconstruction of the longship Skuldelev 5. (© Viking Ship Museum, Roskilde)

5. Orkesta runestone U 344, Sweden. (Berig/Wikimedia Commons)

6. Restitution of lands and liberties to Abingdon, 993. British Library, London, MS Cotton Augustus ii. 38 f.1. (© British Library Board. All Rights Reserved/Bridgeman Images)

7. Silver penny of Æthelred, minted in London, c.1003. Fitzwilliam Museum, Cambridge, MEC 8.1941. (Fitzwilliam Museum, University of Cambridge/Bridgeman Images)

8. Silver penny of Æthelred, minted in Derby in 1009. British Museum, London, 1955,0708.81. (© Trustees of the British Museum)

9. Cissbury Ring, Sussex. (Angelo Hornak/Alamy)

10. Old Sarum, Wiltshire. (De Agostini/Bridgeman Images)

11. Execution burial at St John's College, Oxford. (© Thames Valley Archaeological Services)

12. King Sweyn 'Forkbeard', from Matthew Paris, *Vita S. Eduardi, regis et confessoris*, Cambridge University Library, MS Ee.3.59, fol 4r. (© Syndics of Cambridge University Library)

13. Wulfstan's 'Sermon of the Wolf', early eleventh century. British Library, London, Cotton Nero A.I, f. 110 (© British Library Board. All Rights Reserved/Bridgeman Images)

14. King Æthelred, from *The History of the Church of Abingdon*, *c.*1220. British Library, London, Cotton Claudius B. VI, f.87v. (© British Library Board. All Rights Reserved/Bridgeman Images)

Acknowledgements

In writing *Æthelred the Unready* I drew upon the knowledge and wisdom of friends and colleagues. If the book has errors, it is not because I was *unræd*. I am particularly indebted to Nicole Marafioti and Jill Fitzgerald for reading and critiquing several chapters, and to my fellow biographer Ryan Lavelle, who read the penultimate draft of the book in search of factual errors. I am grateful to Simon Keynes, Rory Naismith and Mary Rambaran-Olm for sharing the fruits of their research. Discussions with Chris Lewis, Steven Isaac, Mary Frances Giandrea and Richard Ruth helped me think through problems of content and structure. The book has greatly benefited from my copy-editor Kate Parker's painstaking attention to detail, insightful queries and suggestions. Above all, I owe thanks to my wife Ellen. Ellen read and commented on each draft of the book and listened patiently as I obsessed about things that happened a thousand years ago. It is to Ellen, my best friend and my best editor, that I dedicate this book.

Index